99

8

A MONTH
WITH
STARFISH

BEV JACKSON

ISBN-10: 1523243163
ISBN-13: 978-1523243167

This book is dedicated to Melinda McRostie of The Captain's Table in Molyvos Harbour, Lesvos, who founded Starfish. Driven by compassion for the refugees who arrived on her doorstep, she set about taking care of them. She created a flexible group of disciplined volunteers that was ideally suited to responding to the daily changes in the influx of refugees. Meanwhile, she carried on running her fine restaurant.

It is also dedicated to the remarkable couple Eric and Philippa Kempson, who gave up their life as artists to care for the refugees who arrive on the beach near their home.

Above all, it is dedicated to the hundreds of thousands of refugees whose lives have been made perilous or unbearable, who have often lost their homes and their loved ones, and who have set out, with heavy hearts, in search of refuge in Europe. Whatever part of Europe they end up enriching, I hope they find there some of the love and kindness that are embodied by Starfish.

BEV JACKSON

ACKNOWLEDGMENTS

Many people contributed to this book. In addition to the tireless efforts of graphic designer Tessa Rose Jackson (TRJ Illustration) and editor Peter Houck, several people kindly took the time to read the manuscript and to make detailed comments: in particular, Marinca Kaldeway, Chris Holloway, Emma Jackson, and Doena van der Vorm. I am very grateful to them. The text benefited enormously from their incisive criticism.

I also want to add a special word of thanks to Heleen, Emma and Tessa for supporting me while I obsessed over this project for months.

I am grateful to Suleman Akhtar for kindly allowing me to quote from his blog.

Finally, I want to thank all my fellow Starfish, the Greek and Spanish lifeguards, the Greek fishermen, all the other volunteers and the refugees I met for reminding me of the true face of human courage and decency. "Thank you for existing," as my friend Omar would say. This was one of the best and most memorable months of my life.

PRELUDE

"Lesvos? Oh, Lesbos! That's a Greek island, isn't it? I thought you were going to India!"

"Mmm, I know, there's been a slight change of plan."

"What's the weather like there in November?"

"We're not going for the weather. But now that you mention it, quite nice actually."

"Lesbos. Isn't that where all those illegal immigrants have been arriving? Is that why you're going?"

"Refugees, you mean. Well, yes. I thought it might be a good idea to help out a bit."

"Aren't you rather old to be wading into the water and pulling people out of boats? And what about your hip?"

"I can always sort clothes. Or clean up. Clear away plastic bottles and life jackets from the beaches, that sort of thing. I bought one of those old people's pick-up gadgets."

"You're not going to be a disaster tourist, are you? What was that thing you said the other day, that the most important thing about helping is –?"

"– Do no harm. The first principle is to do no harm. Anyway, I'm not going to stand around or get in the way. Heleen and I are going together. We're going to sign up with an organization. They'll tell us what needs to be done and we'll do it."

"I thought you really needed a holiday!"

"We can see the Taj Mahal some other time."

"I suppose it's quite noble."

"No it's not. I think I'll feel better if I do something to help than if I just go off and do the tourist thing."

"Oh, I get it!"

"What do you get?"

"You're doing it for yourself. To make yourself feel better, I mean."

"Well, partly, yes. What's wrong with that? Isn't that why people do most things – to make themselves feel better? Why they become a doctor or a nurse? Teach disadvantaged children? The best things I've ever done, I did to make myself feel better. I certainly thought it would make me feel better to have children. And look at them! Best thing I ever did!"

"You always go off on such a tangent."

"Everything's connected."

"I suppose it is. Well, have a good month, then."

"Thanks."

1. THROUGH THE SCREEN

On the scale from saintly to satanic, I bumble along around the midway mark, as I guess most people probably do. I'm married. Heleen and I have a nice apartment. I work at home, translating and crafting sentences. A few times a day I take the dogs out and talk to other dog owners in the park. I spend time with my family, go to the gym, and play tennis. Occasionally we go to a movie, have friends over, or eat out in a restaurant. I support a few charities.

I also watch the news. I watch the news *a lot*. The news happens "over there," on the other side of a TV or computer screen. I am "over here," on this side, in my nice apartment. "Over there" are people whose lives have been ruined by the financial crisis in Greece, people whose loved ones have been lost in a natural disaster, and people whose entire neighbourhoods have been bombed to rubble and who have set off in search of a safe place to live.

It's very sad. It seems as if everything is always mismanaged. Sometimes I get furious and shout abuse at the screen, cursing at the people who constantly make the wrong decisions. Then I switch the TV off and take the dogs out.

I was quite the political activist when I was young, supporting the anti-Apartheid movement and gay rights. Then life happened. I turned my attention to raising my children and earning enough money to pay for music lessons and holidays.

I worked insanely hard in 2015. As summer approached I was looking forward to our annual break. Unusually, we had both freed up an entire month. We would see the Taj Mahal, tour Rajasthan and visit Varanasi before ending up in Nepal for ten days' relaxation.

In April, a terrible earthquake struck Nepal. Over 9,000 people lost their lives. Hundreds of buildings, including some of the most famous temples, collapsed into ruins. It was a calamity for the people of Nepal. I saw the images of devastation and found myself wondering if it would mean that our trip would be cancelled. I watched the horrible events unfold on my TV screen. Then I switched off and took the dogs out.

Meanwhile, wars raged in several Middle Eastern and African countries at once. Millions of people were displaced. The European Union held meetings. With so many people in urgent need of help, the EU's answer was to offer Turkey money and inducements to keep the refugees out. I felt ashamed of Europe. I swore at the TV. Then I switched off and took the dogs out.

In fact, our trip to India and Nepal was cancelled because it was undersubscribed. To my surprise, I felt an enormous sense of relief. As images of war-driven refugees continued to flood from my screens to my mind I had been experiencing an unusual and growing need to step through the screen to the "other side," to stop watching and – for the first time for many years – to make some small physical and personal contribution to a cause beyond my own back yard. I had no illusions about my limitations, but I had read that there were useful things I could do. I could help with clothes and food, or pick up stuff, for instance. Masses of volunteers were gathering to fill the gaps left by unwilling governments and unresponsive aid agencies. I wanted to go and join them.

"Let's go to Greece – to Lesvos," I said to Heleen. To my delight, she immediately, enthusiastically, agreed.

I put my Hindi books back in the bookcase and got out my Greek ones again. I downloaded an audio course in Arabic so that I could communicate with the refugees a little. That was the easy bit. Languages – that's what I understand best.

A few days later the phone rang. It was a fellow translator who had heard about our new plan.

"What are you two really going to do?"

she asked, sounding a bit perplexed.

"Probably do some sorting out, I think. Maybe help to clear plastic water bottles off the paths," I answered, falling back on one of the vague images I had formed.

The contents of our bag told a different story. Aside from the pick-up gadgets and an assortment of items for the refugees – rain suits and ponchos, men's and women's underwear, simple medical supplies, toothbrushes, babies' bottles, toys, and drawing materials – I had packed a high-visibility vest, rain boots, binoculars, two headlamps, two flashlights, and two whistles. Somewhere at the back of my mind, I evidently thought we might be going to the beaches after all.

The beaches. I had been watching the TV images for weeks, for months. More and more desperate refugees were escaping from war, especially in Syria. People were dying in their own countries, but were unable to earn a living or get schooling for their children in the surrounding countries. To have any chance of a life for themselves and their children, they saw no option but to get to Europe. So they made their way to the Mediterranean beaches of North Africa and Turkey. They crammed themselves into small wooden boats and tiny inflatable rubber dinghies that were propelled by less-than-reliable outboard motors. They braved the sea, which many of them had never seen before. It was a perilous journey across the water to Europe, and more than a few people, often children, were drowning every week.

Since the sea routes to Italy were now being patrolled more vigorously, people were flocking to the Greek islands instead. Once in Europe, they could claim asylum as refugees under the 1951 Geneva Convention. In some cases, entire extended families travelled together. Often the eldest son would go alone, partly to avoid being drafted into the army to fight his fellow countrymen and partly to find a refuge where the rest of the family might be able to join him later.

Unfortunately, Europe had not created a legal way for them to get there. There was no safe and cheap passage on the ferries and cruise ships that "normal" travellers could take. When something is urgently needed but can't be done legally, criminals fill the gap. So, as has been the case for centuries, a lively smuggling trade had grown up. For part of the journey, refugees would have to place their lives in the hands of the people smugglers. Europe had spawned a totally unregulated international transport industry.

This industry, the business of buying the flimsy wooden boats and rubber dinghies and transporting the desperate to Europe, was almost entirely in the hands of Turkey's organized crime syndicates. The business model was simple: extract maximum money from the migrants. Safety was not a consideration. Bad weather would sometimes mean discounted ticket prices. If someone balked at boarding a boat in rough seas or felt that the boat was dangerously overloaded, a gun or knife might be held to his head until he gave in. One of the passengers, maybe boarding a boat for the first time in his life, was placed at the helm, given two minutes of instruction, and told to head "that way" towards Greece. The smuggler would then simply jump off the boat to prepare the next batch of travellers. Luggage was frequently tossed overboard in order to cram even more passengers into the little boats. The Turkish boat mafia was earning millions, and still is, by transporting people to the nearest point of the European Union.

The distance from Turkey to the closest landing place on the north coast of Lesvos is just four and a half miles. In 2015, thousands of refugees were arriving on Lesvos every day. On some October days over 7,000 refugees came off boats onto the rocky beaches of an island with a population of only 89,000. Once they came ashore they needed dry clothes, food, water, information, comfort. Greece, its economy already wrecked, couldn't cope.

As the exodus accelerated, around the planet people of all nationalities and from all walks of life watched their TV screens in disbelief and reached the same conclusion that we had: "Go to Lesvos!" My friend Peter would later describe the growth of the volunteer effort on Lesvos and the other Greek islands as an organic, anarchic convergence – ordinary people taking care of things themselves. "People came from all over the world in response to a non-official call for help, as if drawn by a scent or a pheromone released by an injured plant or a chemotactic factor from a damaged organ."

The name "Eftalou" kept appearing in news reports; it was the closest landing beach to Turkey. A quick check of the atlas found Eftalou close to Molyvos, one of the most beautiful villages in the Aegean islands. My daughter Emma, who had visited Molyvos a few years before, was excited at this coincidence and mentioned a particularly good restaurant at the harbour. I googled it and discovered that by an additional astonishing coincidence this restaurant, The Captain's Table, run by Melinda McRostie and her husband Theo, had become the headquarters of a volunteer organization set up to help the refugees. It was called Starfish. We registered online and said we would be coming for a month. Our course was set.

2. IN TRANSIT

I love Greece and had flown there many times before. This time, however, I was not relaxing into my holiday reading but trying to clear my head, which was buzzing with scraps of possible scenarios in a strange in-between land. I had no idea how I was going to spend the next month. That was exciting, but also unnerving.

Because we were travelling to Lesvos out of season, there were no direct flights and we had to change at Munich and Athens. I caught myself internally grumbling about the long stopover time and shook the thought off: how much simpler was my journey south than the journey north being undertaken, partly on foot, by thousands of people below our flight path?

I knew the lovely island of Lesvos a little, from a visit many years before. But what awaited me there now? Going by the images I had seen and the reports I had heard, the sheer numbers of arrivals, I imagined a kind of war zone, with lines of desperate people stumbling along the roads, piles of orange life jackets everywhere, and a seething brouhaha between islanders and newcomers.

During our time in transit at Athens airport we did the usual travel things: had some non-airline food, bought and installed Greek SIM cards, and the like. It still seemed a lot like a standard holiday. However, I was very conscious that this was no holiday. As we waited to board the plane to Lesvos I looked around, trying to guess which of my fellow passengers were also going to volunteer. I sat down and started chatting to the woman beside me, Lindsay, an outgoing young woman with a cheerful manner. She was a medical social worker from Virginia. Her IT husband would be taking time off work to care for their young sons while she was away. She had asked him to consider this volunteering trip her Christmas present.

Many members of Lindsay's local community had donated goods for her to take along for the refugees. Lindsay had asked United Airlines about the three extra cases she would be bringing on the flight. UA said there would be an extra charge of $300, but that a note from her organization could get that waived at the gate. At the airport, UA not only disregarded the note, but told her the extra charge would be $500, rather than the $300 she'd been quoted online and over the phone, saying: "If you don't want to pay, you can just leave everything behind."

Lindsay asked to see the manager, who just happened to be within earshot and came over to add: "We can't be expected to help every humanitarian aid worker who comes through here. Next time give us twelve months' notice and we might be able to help," before striding away. Knowing that her suitcases carried much-needed medical supplies, she sat in shock over her poor treatment for a few minutes, then just paid up and proceeded to her gate.

The story made me furious, and I decided never to fly UA again. Our own experience had been very different. We had brought one extra piece of luggage containing items for the refugees. Lufthansa waived the charge.

I greeted another, older woman as she joined the line to board the plane. She spoke French, and when she heard I was going to help, she demanded to know "How?"

I said I didn't know. "Perhaps unpack and sort clothes." I didn't mention cleaning up plastic bottles.

She exclaimed quite angrily, "But that's not the solution!" as if she thought I ought to be meeting up with Putin instead. Perhaps she was a politician. Not a journalist, I thought, since she did not speak a word of English. I wanted to ask her what she was going to do on Lesvos but she was already boarding.

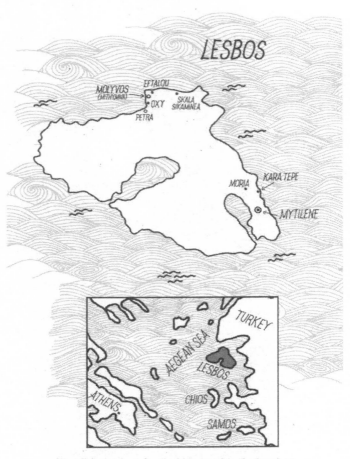

The distance from the Turkish coast to the beach at
Eftalou is about 4½ miles.

3. TO MOLYVOS

Lesvos is one of the largest islands in the Aegean. From the airport of Mytilene in the southeast of the island it was a 42-mile drive to Molyvos. Since it was late we had booked a taxi, planning to rent a car the next day. Our Australian driver spoke non-stop in a tour guide's spiel about the island, his English so fast that I found myself missing whole sections. We tried to turn the conversation to the refugee situation but he preferred to keep to his standard chat: "There are 11 million olive trees on this island," he told us. We missed the last few million because it was pitch dark as we climbed and then descended through one increasingly tight hairpin bend after another. For whatever reason, fear of automotive death or preoccupations about what lay ahead, the rest of his chatter washed over me – until he got to the part about the lesbians.

"Now, lesbians, I have no problem with the ladies, not at all, but they have nothing to do with Lesvos, that's a total mix up, I don't know how that happened. The spelling is different. Lesvos is spelt with a "v," it has nothing to do with lesbians."

I thought that was funny. The word "lesbian," of course, does derive from the name of the island of Lesbos/Lesvos, because the great Greek poet Sappho, who wrote love poems about women, was born in Eressos, in the southwest of the island. Still, once in a blue moon someone will get hot under the collar about the word. Like the man who instituted a curious legal battle in 2008 to get the "Gay and Lesbian Community of Greece" to change its name. "Only people from Lesbos are Lesbian" appears to have been his argument. Anyway, he lost the case.

Dropping down the far side of the island's divide the curvatures of the road gradually eased. Ahead a few miles and to our left was the sea, betrayed by a scattering of ships' lamps. As our tour guide cheerfully announced "About three miles from Molyvos!" we rounded a bend and a ghostly white patch of land emerged from the darkness. Our driver slowed a little as we passed a rocky parking lot. We saw tents, dimly lit by bare fluorescent lights. A big white tent looked more like a barn with its door gaping open towards us. In front of it and near a ragged cluster of small mountaineering tents that trailed off into the darkness, groups of people stood around.

"That's Oxy," said our driver. "It's a kind of camp." It looked depressing.

Our taxi dived back into the darkness beyond the camp's island of light and swung around another bend to the right. There before us, silhouetted in the distance against the night sky, rose the village of Molyvos. A breathtaking sight. Little stone houses climb up all around the central hill. Cresting the top is the ancient fortress, illuminated at night, like a shimmering fairytale castle. To our right this glowing spectacle, and to our left the dark water of the bay. Although we could not see it, we knew that Turkey lay just a few miles away, across that stretch of water.

A few minutes later we arrived at Nadia's Apartments, just before and below the village's steep cobblestoned streets. Hearing our taxi arrive, Nadia herself came out to greet us. She turned out to be the driver's cousin. The complex consisted of attractive renovated stone houses set in a garden with fruit trees all around. We immediately warmed to Nadia's friendly and engaging manner. Whatever we said, she replied, "Don't worry!" with such depth of feeling that it seemed as if we could not possibly have anything to worry about ever again.

While we were settling in, someone came to the door. The Dutch volunteers in the next apartment were packing up to go home. They told us a little about their work on the beaches and said how hard they found it to leave. This was something we were to hear from almost everyone who left. Our Dutch neighbours offered us their unused supplies.

Ten minutes later came another knock on the door. Nadia had brought us cake for next day's breakfast.

4. THE CAPTAIN'S TABLE

In the morning we walked about fifteen minutes along the narrow coastal road that clung to the top of a cliff dropping into the sea, past shops and now quiet eateries, to the harbour. We had to report for an induction meeting with Starfish.

We went down the cobblestone path that opens out into a harbour enveloped by two convex stretches of jetty, with a long line of fishing boats, some large and others tiny with bright red and blue paint. Clearly, it was a working harbour, not just a set in a touristic fantasy. There, in the crook of the harbour's arms was the restaurant, The Captain's Table, its outside area covered with tables stretching the twenty yards to the water's edge. To one side, dangling from a line slung between two posts, octopus tentacles had been hung out to dry. Beside them was a board with different dangling things. I looked more closely. These were cables for iPhones and Androids. The board was a charging station for the refugees. Almost all refugees, even those who arrive penniless and whose luggage has been tossed overboard by the people smugglers, have mobile phones, often wrapped in foil or plastic to keep dry. It is their lifeline, to tell relatives and friends that they are safe and to find information for their journey.

Although we encountered several volunteers on the path, we had not yet seen a single refugee. Nor had we seen any of the rubbish or chaos I had imagined beforehand. It was a serene October morning in one of the finest tourist destinations in the Aegean. In a mood of mild exhilaration we climbed the three steps into the small indoor seating area of the Captain's Table, the volunteer nerve centre of Starfish.

We sat around a table with three other new volunteers. Two were German women in their forties, who spoke their sons' names proudly as a badge of honour: the two cousins had worked tirelessly for Starfish over the summer, and their mothers were now following in their footsteps. The third was a young Dutch girl. The volunteer manager Trace, one of the impressive core group of Starfish volunteers, prepared us with a wide-ranging description of the task ahead. She had given up her job as a youth worker in the north of England to help here. Trace struck me as someone with a rare brand of wisdom, who quickly intuits what is important, dresses it in benevolence, and dismisses trivia without a second thought. She spoke softly and carefully as she told us how Starfish worked and explained the arrangements at Oxy transit area, the ghostly nocturnal apparition we had passed the night before. Oxy was run by Starfish. It was a brief stopping point for refugees to obtain food and dry clothing, to rest and get medical help if needed before heading south to the main camps near Mytilene. Refugees stayed anywhere from a few hours to a few nights at Oxy, depending on the flow of refugees, which varied greatly from one day to the next.

Trace also sketched a far broader context, warning us against making certain grave mistakes: "Do no harm." She pointed out the importance of remaining calm, especially on the beach. At this point, visions of cleaning up plastic bottles receded further from my mind. "A lot of cheerful welcomes can actually raise the anxiety level," she continued. Trace described what a long line of waving people on the beach must look like to an anxious person who finds himself at the helm of a boat for the first time in his life, responsible for the lives of some fifty other people. The sight may confuse him and actually cause him to make mistakes. Calmly allowing him to make his own way in to shore is often better. "Cheers and shouts of welcome may be harmful too." A refugee might leap happily out of his boat, only to break his ankle, landing on the rocks!

She warned us never to answer questions, however much we might want to be helpful, unless we were absolutely sure of the answers. These answers – which countries are doing what, for instance – might change from one day to the next. It was vital not to spread misinformation. She also cautioned that so many things are not what they seem, citing as an example a volunteer who had been filmed shouting at a line of refugees who were preparing to board a bus. Once the cameras had gone and everyone was on the bus, the refugees all applauded her for getting it done in such an orderly way. But that part was not filmed, so that the outside world was left with the image of a bossy volunteer ordering the refugees about. It was a reminder that we were now on "the other side" of the world's screens. Another warning was to be careful about asking refugees what had happened to them. Some of them had been forced to repeat and relive traumatic events so often that it added to their distress.

As Trace was talking to us, a young man who spoke only Arabic interrupted the meeting to show us all a photo of someone he was trying to find. He appeared terribly worried, so I looked around to give him a glass of water. I assumed that he was a refugee who had lost one of his relatives.

"He's one of us!" said a woman who had just emerged from the restaurant kitchen, staring at me. The worried man was a member of the volunteer team.

The woman who had spoken to me was Melinda McRostie, who owns The Captain's Table together with her husband Theo. An unassuming presence who conveys the impression of keeping arm's-length but effective control behind the scenes, she tends to shrug her shoulders when people exclaim about the miracle she has performed here. She set up this organization of volunteers when refugees started arriving on her doorstep and it was obvious that something had to be done to help them. When she is asked why she took this task upon herself, she quotes the Starfish story, a popular folk tale.

The Starfish Story

> A little girl walking by the beach sees thousands of starfish washed up on shore and begins throwing them back into the sea. An old man sees her and asks why — there are far too many starfish for her to rescue by herself. The little girl picks up a starfish and holds it up: "I've saved this one."

I noticed a young boy begging outside the restaurant tables. "A refugee?" I again thought. Again, no. It turned out that he was a local Greek boy. I was starting to learn an essential lesson: to be aware of my bad habit of jumping to conclusions.

After the induction talk, we picked up our rental car and drove to see Oxy by daylight. We did not yet realize how much of our month on Lesvos would be spent at this oddly named outpost – it was located in the parking lot of the adjacent Oxy night club. The club, jutting from the hillside above the road and looking a bit tired and rundown in the off season, was closed, at least temporarily.

Oxy, sprawling beside a main road and four miles from the beach, looked more brown and soil-beige in daylight than the grey, black, and white of the previous night. But there were more signs of life in the light. We saw dazed-looking men and women, and many children. At least the children were playing, as children seem to do in almost any circumstances. This sad space was the only place that could be agreed with the authorities for the wet and exhausted refugees to receive some brief elementary care before boarding buses to Mytilene, the island's capital. If there was a backlog or the buses didn't come, they would have to sleep here.

The small tents looked a bit more colourful in daylight, and the gaping entrance to the large tent did not look nearly as fearsome as it had in the dark. We were told that sometimes people would be obliged to sleep out in the open air. This was bad enough in fair weather. And then if it rained...

Sometimes there were no buses and newcomers had to walk to Oxy from the beach. We stood for a while watching the volunteers in the ticket booth give people coloured cards with pictures for the buses to Mytilene (the tickets for one bus were pink with a picture of a smiley, for instance, while those for the next bus were green with a banana). Syrian families boarded one bus, everyone else would be assigned to a different one. This struck a raw nerve with some of the Afghans. It was unavoidable, though, as the refugees had separate camps in the south of the island: Syrian families went to Kara Tepe, others to Moria.

Keeping all this running was a lot of work. Starfish needed over twenty different jobs done, including making sandwiches, handing out tickets, distributing food, dispensing clothes, helping people to board buses, cleaning, and keeping the youngest kids occupied in the children's tent. Two wonderful Greek people cleaned the toilets, and at night there were Greek security guards in army fatigues. Others helped on the beach, unpacked donations, and transported people and goods around our part of the island. Most of this was 24/7.

Shifts were from 7 a.m. to 3:30 p.m., from 3 p.m. to 11:30 p.m., and from 11 p.m. to 7:30 a.m. I had said I was too old to do the night shift, and didn't allow myself to feel guilty about it. I wondered how I would cope with shifts of eight and a half hours without a break. I'd never done it before. At home I work hard, but I normally take breaks throughout the day.

For three shifts a day they needed about ninety volunteers. Today there were twenty-five. Heleen and I had planned to take the first weekend off, to get our bearings, but that was clearly impossible. We agreed to start the next morning, making sandwiches.

5. SANDWICHES AND SMOKE

As we reached the harbour at 9 a.m. the next day, we were about to ask Trace for directions to the sandwich factory when we saw that she was bending forward and commiserating with a middle-aged man with a tufty grey beard. He reminded me a little of the American poet Alan Ginsberg. It turned out that our "Ginsberg" was German and had slight difficulties with the English-based WhatsApp, the mobile phone app through which we communicated with fellow volunteers. He had turned up to make sandwiches at 7 a.m. and since the key was not where it should have been, he had been pacing around the harbour for two hours. He was distressed and a bit out of sorts.

The three of us headed up a narrow lane to the "sandwich factory," a little stone house up the hillside from the harbour. Ginsberg gradually ungrumped. We had an industrious shift inserting two slices of processed cheese (or "cheese product," some might say) between slices of gooey processed white bread and then cramming the whole lot back into the bags that the bread had come in. I heard that a variation had been tried for a while, putting one slice of turkey and one slice of cheese in each sandwich instead of two slices of cheese, but some of the refugees had mistaken the turkey for pork and refused to eat it. Double slices of cheese were deemed safest. Then there had been the person who sweetly suggested that we use better cheese and whole wheat bread, until it was pointed out that Starfish's food budget was already astronomic and it simply couldn't be done. All in all, the food was not very elegant and probably not very healthy, but it was the best Starfish could do.

Each of us arranged the bread and cheese in different ways. I kept peeking at Ginsberg's and Heleen's systems to see if they looked more efficient than mine. A discussion arose as to whether each pack had to contain fourteen or fifteen sandwiches.

Occasionally an elderly Greek man entered the house through the front door, walked past the rooms where we were working, and out through the back door. We nodded in greeting. It was a neighbour, taking the quickest route back to his home. When we finished our shift, the fridges were full and we felt satisfied with our first day's work as Starfish volunteers.

Our "firsts" continued. In the middle of the day, three dinghies sailed straight from Turkey into Molyvos harbour rather than landing on the beaches. The people were not rescued by the coastguard, but had simply steered right across into the harbour. Evidently someone knew exactly what he was doing, because this nautical feat required navigating around the hook of headland on the far northwest corner of the island. This was very unusual. They moored neatly at the quayside, a hundred people or so, waved and said "hello!" Since they had not been rescued, we did not need to register them here at the harbour – that was the rule – and they set off to walk to Oxy.

I sat drinking coffee at Captain's Table after my shift, watching the new refugee arrivals and the volunteers around me. I became aware of a man sitting at a table. He had an unapproachable, inward expression. His whole presence was vaguely troubling and didn't seem to fit with the generally happy demeanour of the volunteers I had seen that morning. It was only later, when I had seen several more people with a similar fixed stare, and spoken to one of them, that I understood. I had read of the terrible shipwreck that had taken place just outside the harbour on 28 October, two days before our arrival. An old wooden boat, no longer seaworthy, had been crammed with over three hundred refugees. The rickety top deck had collapsed onto the lower deck under the sheer weight of the refugees. Some people had been crushed, while others drowned, trapped below deck as the ship keeled over and sank. The Greek coast-guard and other vessels had rescued as many people as they could, but casualties were high. As these hundreds of soaking, shocked people were brought ashore, the entire village opened their homes to them. Everywhere, refugees had been taken in and given dry clothes and food. Meanwhile, on the jetty and on the ground outside the restaurants, doctors, nurses, and volunteers with no medical training tried to resuscitate dozens of refugees who showed little sign of life. Many of these victims were children. We never found out the exact number of people who perished that night, but it might have been as many as fifty.

When I saw that fixed, inward look, I came to recognize it as someone remembering his attempts to save a refugee, perhaps a child, and seeing the limp body eventually covered up and taken away. The man I spoke to did not want to talk about it. He was obviously distraught. A few days later, a psychologist came to our Starfish meeting to talk to the volunteers who had been involved in the dramatic rescue and to offer counselling, but the distraught man had already left to fly home. I wondered how many volunteers would be experiencing post-traumatic stress syndrome and whether they would all find the care they needed.

That evening we had dinner at a local restaurant. The owner sat smoking at the next table. I had already been struck by how many people smoked here: islanders, refugees, and Greek and foreign volunteers alike. Normally I find the presence of smoke pretty unbearable but here I soon discovered that it didn't bother me. It was as if my body had made a quick calculation – refugees fleeing from death, volunteers dealing with stressful situations –

and concluded that it was ridiculous to fuss about smoking when people's lives were at stake. Normally it made me feel ill, and now it didn't.

6. THE FOOD TENT

After a day at the sandwich factory I was put on shift at Oxy, handing out food. Starfish had organized the oddly-shaped sprawl of the parking lot into a functional camp. There was one large tent, provided by the UNHCR (the United Nations Refugee Agency), along with a few smaller tents and several plastic Ikea huts that we also called "tents": one for handing out tickets for the bus to Mytilene, one for food distribution, a medical tent, a children's tent, and tents for women's and men's clothes.

First port of call for the refugees was the ticket tent.

"Hello! Welcome! Where are you from? Iraq? OK! How many people? *Khamsa*? Right, here are five bus tickets. And these tickets are for food! Here is the map of the island. We are now *here* and the bus will take you *there*. To *Mytilene*. Then you can register with the police

31

and buy a ticket for the boat to Athens. Good luck!"

It was amazing how soon I began to see this scraggly stretch of dust and stones as a cocoon of kindness. Although my first impression of Oxy had been of a dreary wasteland, I soon came to feel attached to it – no, to *love* it.

At the food tent, I was distributing the sandwiches I had packed the day before – in principle, the ration was just one a day for each person – along with a piece of fruit and unlimited water. Of course, since this was only a transit camp, most people would not be staying for longer than a few hours. It soon became clear that we accepted that some people would keep fetching extra tickets and coming back for more food.

My emotions were still close to the surface. The first time a man looked into my eyes and said: "you really good people!" I teared up a little. I remember our eyes locking, his eyes looking out from his situation and mine looking back from mine. The intensity of this exchange struck me with great force. These eye-conversations throughout that first day were also exhausting. Unconsciously, I retreated emotionally; it seems I had to, in order to function well.

"Where you from?" said another refugee.

"Holland" I said.

"Ah, Arjen Robben" he said, and we smiled at the famous soccer player's name. Once upon a time it was the name of Johan Cruyff, the soccer mega-star of the 1970s, that would be invoked.

Then a man came and gave back his family's three bananas and three sandwiches and three bottles of water. Puzzled, I thought he had received too much by mistake so I put them away. Then he asked for a plastic bag and I thought it a more than fair exchange. Perhaps I was getting a bit tired. Finally I understood that he needed the bag to put his food in, and I gave it all back, in a bag. I laughed at the misunderstanding and so did he. We both cracked up laughing.

By 8 p.m. I was feeling drained. Still three and a half hours to go, and I was starting to panic.

"Your energy level is definitely flagging," was the concise verdict of Kirsten, who would become a good friend. I appreciate bluntness. It's reassuring.

A Greek couple brought bananas. We already had too many but I took my cue from my fellow workers: we were always grateful when locals came and donated food. The couple wanted to go round handing them out to children, but two buses had just left and at that moment there weren't many people in camp. Eventually they left the bananas at the food tent and went home.

The next morning I went to the pharmacy to buy more hand sanitizer. We were going through pints of the stuff at the food tent. There was something about the pharmacist's shoulders that reminded me of a florist near my house in Amsterdam. A rather Scrooge-like person, with so much melancholy poured into his bones that it could never get out.

The pharmacist sketched to me his view of the future.

"When all this is finished," he nodded, looking steadily into his dark mirror, "Refugees gone, volunteers gone," Then he nodded again, agreeing with himself, "Then the tourists too will all be gone, and the island will be dead," he concluded.

I tried to introduce a brighter, more buoyant, note, pointing out that the extraordinary character of the islanders and the beauty of his village were now in the limelight as never before, but soon gave up. I wondered if I was going to meet many people who were this glum. In fact, the pharmacist was by far the most miserable person I met all month. I went out from his sad shop into glorious sunshine, and felt – knew – that he was wrong. Lesvos would always be a great place for a holiday!

7. HALIB!

Now came my first really hard day's work. To ward off the alarming fatigue that had weighed me down the day before I had brought bags of high-energy food (to be eaten out of sight of the refugees, to avoid aggravating their hunger): glucose tablets, chocolate, and bananas. I spent the morning writing down the previous day's experiences and after lunch I was back at the "food tent."

I had a gruelling shift, on my feet from 3 till 11 pm. For the first four or five hours the lines were endless. We had no time to go to the toilet or drink water. Two of us staffed the food tent, with one handing out food and water and the other keeping the boxes filled and ordering more on our WhatsApp group communication channel when needed. At 7 p.m. I took a five-minute break. From 8 till 11 p.m. the numbers waiting in line gradually declined. News came in on the app of another boat sinking, another child drowned, maybe more. We read the news quickly, but had no time to digest it. We went back to serving our customers.

Handing out food went like this. Three people would crowd around the window, waving tickets. The one who seemed to be first in line said "Family!" and handed over his bundle of scraps of paper that he had been given at the ticket hut. I counted. There were fifteen.

We gave him his big bag of sandwiches, another bag of apples (the day before we had had too many bananas, now we had too few), a third of water. Then he said *halib!* which means milk.

"You have babies?" we asked, babies being our word for children.

When he understood, he held up three fingers, and we gave him three cups of milk.

The next man had a bigger family and handed over twenty-one tickets. He had one of his relatives there to help him, which was essential, especially with the *halib.*

Then came a smaller family with two girls. The elder daughter, about ten years old, strode up to the window and asked for her family's sandwiches, fruit and drinks in excellent English. She flashed a smile at me when I complimented her, and I asked her what she wanted to be when she grew up.

"A doctor!" she said, beaming.

"And your sister?" I asked.

"Oh, she wants to be a fashion designer," she said, in a neutral voice.

I said I thought they would be an excellent doctor and fashion designer. Their parents looked proud but very tired. They did not speak English.

Later on a girl aged about fifteen came to the food tent. She said she was travelling alone with four younger siblings. I wondered if I had understood correctly. I wished her good luck, which seemed pretty inadequate. It was so busy. Her face preyed on my mind, and I berated myself for not checking that someone had been alerted to their predicament in order to provide additional support.

One big man arrived, like many other Syrians full of exasperation at having to make this journey.

"But what do you do when your government are killers?" he exclaimed as he took his ration: one sandwich, a piece of fruit and a bottle of water for each person in his family.

The food bill was thousands of euros every day. Starfish pays for all the food it distributes from private donations. It receives no money from the EU, the Greek government, or major aid agencies.

At 7 o'clock, blankets were handed out, as it was getting cold.

The IRC (International Rescue Committee, an agency whose CEO is David Miliband) was responsible for transporting the refugees to the camps in Mytilene. But no more buses were expected that day. Maybe the camps were full, so people would have to sleep at Oxy. Two hundred could fit in the big UNHCR tent, perhaps another hundred in the smaller tents, and the rest on the rocks in the open air. In total about 950 people would sleep at Oxy that night. Thank God it wasn't raining!

One man lay down against the door to the food tent so we couldn't get out. Someone outside had to wake him up and move him. Most people settled down around 10 p.m. Here and there a baby wailed. A middle-aged woman kept coming back and demanding more food, and we had to say no. One ticket, one ration. Except I would occasionally give more to someone very old and frail, and to children travelling alone.

8. FERRY STRIKE

I covered the car seats with thick garbage bags in case I would be giving refugees a lift on the four mile walk to Oxy. People often arrive very wet from the boats, and some of the car hire companies charge steep rates for chemical cleaning. On the way to my shift I passed two men walking alone, and decided not to take them, because maybe I would pass someone whose need was greater. Then I passed a group of eight people, with one child. I decided that choosing who to take would cause problems, so ended up taking no one. I felt bad about this, but when I arrived at Oxy and told one of the Norwegian volunteers he said I had been right. "Do no harm"!

The previous day was a warm-up; this was a seriously tough shift. I was back at the food tent, but we were in crisis. The ferries between Mytilene and Athens were on strike, which meant the camps in Mytilene were full. The police had ordered the buses from Oxy to Mytilene to be stopped, so Oxy just got fuller and fuller. Tempers sometimes frayed. The food line stretched almost endlessly; at one point there were about 1,000 people waiting in line, down the road and around the corner. Later one man said he had been standing in line for four hours.

At the front of the line, a small boy stood with his nose squashed against the side of the hut. He looked as if the air was being pressed out of him by the people behind. On the other side, so many people were clamouring to be served that the plastic hut seemed in danger of being cracked open.

I got out my phone and texted a message: "Crowd control please at food tent! Children getting squashed! Tent will break!"

Two minutes later, the redoubtable Maria arrived, and told us to shut the food tent while she set up a crowd control barrier. So we closed the window and retreated into our little hut, ignoring the swelling tumult of frustrated voices outside. We waited while some clever Starfish (including Heleen) created a system that would only allow a few people through at a time. Twenty minutes later we re-opened and the waiting masses had been magically refashioned into an orderly line.

Luckily I was working with Alina, a Romanian woman who used to work at a bank and therefore stayed calm all the time and NEVER LOST COUNT of the sandwiches etc. She said "Hello!" in exactly the same cheerful tone of voice after greeting 1500 people as she did at the beginning of her shift.

"Banana or aypell?" she asked. After hearing her say that hundreds of times, I felt that I had mispronounced the word "apple" all my life.

At the end of our shift, the camp manager came up with some of the others and applauded us for feeding 1500 people on our shift! We took some photos of the entire Starfish group at Oxy.

As I left the food tent at 23:15, I looked around, and in the dark I could see hundreds and hundreds of dark grey mounds, like a huge crop of large stones that had sprouted up in the evening. They were around all the tents and huts, including the toilets, and along both sides of the road. These were the grey blankets we handed out after sunset, and under each one was a person. They were also lying around the place where we parked the cars, which made it nerve-racking to back out, making sure there was no one behind us. In total, 2,200 people slept at Oxy that night. I was so thankful it was not raining.

9. "SO MANY PEOPLE COME AND GO"

Even though the previous day's shift had been stressful, I no longer had energy problems. I pondered why. Perhaps it was partly just a matter of acclimatizing to a new situation; I did not have an energy dip because I had re-tuned to a new schedule. And partly, perhaps, I had unconsciously shut off some of my own emotions as a protective measure. I no longer felt close to tears when I saw vulnerable people struggling along, and just tried to work in an efficient, friendly way.

The next day I had an early shift, starting at 7 a.m., which was a pity coming straight after a late shift. I had only slept for three hours. But luckily I was only making sandwiches, a fairly mindless task. I somehow managed to get lost on my way to the "sandwich factory," even though I had already been there before, on my first day, so I put out a plaintive message on the app:

"Help! I am directionally challenged and can't find the sandwich factory!"

A young Swiss man called Josua immediately called me to give precise directions. When I arrived, I found I was working with a Norwegian woman.

I said, "Hi! I'm Bev," and she said, barely looking up:

"Oh. So many people come and go," which I thought was an inauspicious beginning. She became a little friendlier later on. She used to be a vet and had grown tired of it. Now she works mostly for international agencies, often in developing countries.

After my shift I had a chat with our wonderful landlady, Nadia, a married woman of around thirty-nine with two children. Her catch phrase "Don't worry!" remained comforting. Sometimes we sat outside enjoying the wonderful garden, dotted around with lemon, orange and fig trees laden with fruit, and chickens wandering about among the shrubs. The previous day, Nadia's mother had come to change the sheets and gave us two eggs that she had found in the garden. Nadia expressed great compassion for the refugees, and had none of the pharmacist's pessimism. Still, she agreed that finding a good place to accommodate the new arrivals in the north of the island, the hub of the island's tourism, was difficult. It had been far from ideal when her small children were walking past lines of hundreds of refugees hanging their clothes to dry on the fence outside the entrance to their school every day. She belonged to a group of villagers who got together to pick up rubbish from the beaches every few days, so I lent her my elderly person's pick-up stick gadget and she liked it!

At the end of the afternoon Heleen and I walked up the hill into Molyvos proper, through the maze of steps and winding alleys. Some of the little cafes and shops were still open, others closed for the winter. (Winter? We had brought tons of raingear, but now we needed to buy sunscreen. One of the Norwegians was out in the sun loading buses at Oxy for six hours and went beet red).

We went right up to the top of the hill and walked around the imposing castle, with a view of the entire surrounding countryside. We stayed there for a while and watched the glorious sunset.

10. KEYS, MEDICAL MATTERS, AND POLITICS

I pulled the door shut as we set off for our next shift. Just as Heleen said she had forgotten her phone, I realized I had taken the wrong key. We were locked out, with both keys and Heleen's phone inside, and needed to leave pronto. I realized this was serious when Nadia did not say "Don't worry!" but actually looked worried. Then she fetched her youngest daughter, manoeuvred her in through the bathroom window, and hey presto! I gave the little girl a bag with toy animals I had brought from my grandchildren.

Up the winding road to Oxy, and back to the food tent. I served the people, and Heleen kept the crates of food and water filled. As the day went on, an endless line of people snaked around the camp waiting to get their sandwich and apple or banana. The job reminded me a little of my time working at Melkweg multimedia centre in Amsterdam over forty years ago, facing people whose eyes were bleary for an entirely different reason.

A dispute arose among the volunteers. Someone said that we should hide the apples or bananas because choosing took time and people had to wait longer. I disagreed. These people had so little choice in their lives now, as they went from boat to beach to bus to transit camp to bus to camp to ship and then train or trudging onward through Europe, hoping that borders would stay open. Could they please choose whether to have an apple or a banana? We had two sorts of apples today.

"Apple. Red!" said one man, pointing with pleasure at the ginormous red apples that had just been delivered.

A Syrian man came up to the window holding a carrier in his left hand. I peered over the edge of the counter for a closer look. A cage, with a bright green and yellow bird. A refugee parrot! I took a picture of the parrot and it gazed back at me as it sat quietly in its cage. I wondered how it would get across the borders, if it had the right papers.

Someone came up to the window wearing a face mask with traces of blood on it. Later I went to the medics' tent and asked if this meant that he had infectious tuberculosis.

"It's in the differential," said the doctor. I asked her to tell me other more reassuring things it might mean.

"A nosebleed," she said, "or a bad cough. He is probably protecting himself rather than protecting others." She did add that we should all have ourselves tested for TB after returning home. She would certainly do so.

At 9 o'clock the line ended and we had time for a chat. One of our Farsi interpreters, an outgoing, enthusiastic Iranian refugee, came to our tent and joined in. The conversation ranged across Europe and across the centuries, and at some point we came to the subject of King Darius I of Persia.

"He was quite a cruel king, wasn't he?" I said. The interpreter went white with rage. King Darius was the best king *ever*, and how is it possible that you people don't know about him, and he was the first person to draw up a list of human rights, which is at the United Nations headquarters in New York. The interpreter was almost inconsolable at my ignorance and stupidity about King Darius. I apologized again and again and promised to research King Darius and to spread the word about his excellence.

Then Heleen said to the interpreter,

"And the person we call Alexander the Great, isn't it true that you call him 'Alexander the Terrible?'"

"No, no," he replied. "Alexander killed many Persians but still we call him great. He was great. Hitler was great too! He got many countries."

Silence in the food tent.

Trying to digest this, I said:

"No. He was not great."

Then I added, "I'm Jewish!"

The interpreter looked aghast, and said slowly, "Oh........ shit!"

I went on:

"But the fact that I am Jewish is not so important. Heleen is not Jewish but we feel the same. Someone who kills six million Jews, or six million Muslims, or six million Christians, is not great. That is evil. Most people in Europe think that."

"Really?" said the interpreter.

"Except for fascists," I added.

It was an interesting cultural encounter. We hugged and agreed to revise our opinions about King Darius and about Hitler.

11. TALE OF TWO CAMPS

Heleen and I took the weekend off. We decided to drive to Mytilene, do some shopping, and look at the camps Kara Tepe and Moria. At that time, Kara Tepe was for Syrian families, and Moria was for Afghans and everyone else, including (sometimes) Syrian men travelling without families. We gave a lift to three Canadian volunteers who spoke Arabic. The first half of the road was slow, with lots of hairpin bends, and the second half was straighter, with occasional potholes and stretches under construction. We decided to go to Moria first.

Moria camp is actually easy to find, but since we decided to follow a sign to Moria we got lost and wasted half an hour back-tracking to the road we should have stayed on. As we parked, we saw ramshackle huts lining the road outside. Vendors were selling food, sandals, clothes – all at high prices. We were told there was also a kiosk with little tents for 20 euros. There was a lively black market trade in money. For 100 Turkish lira you could get 20 euros, instead of the real exchange rate, which was closer to 30.

Moria was on the same kind of rocky terrain as Oxy, but it was completely different in several ways. It was huge and filthy. There were thousands of people there, often having to stay for many days waiting to register before they could board a ship to Athens. Most had to sleep in the open air because they couldn't afford to buy a tent. Moria was surrounded by a high fence topped with barbed wire. We met a young Afghan man outside the camp. He spoke English and offered to show us around. He said that back in Afghanistan he had received death threats from the Taliban for working with foreigners, and was therefore now seeking asylum.

Our guide led us towards a gap in the fence that served as an entrance to the camp. We bent down under the barbed wire and went in. Although I knew there were volunteers working here, they were not easy to find. I did not see one volunteer, doctor, or cleaner in the hour I spent at Moria, nor were there any information signs.

Our guide said, "I am very sorry to have to tell you this, but there is a big problem here. No one cleans the toilets."

Heleen went to have a look. The toilets were full of excrement, mud and wet clothes. One man approached them, shrank back at the terrible smell, and went away again.

We walked on. Two men who recognized us from Oxy came and stood near us. One said he had been waiting for days and had no tent. One of his children was sick. I gave him 20 euros for a tent, as furtively as possible. A few minutes later his friend came over and said that his family also had no tent, so I gave him 20 euros as well.

Our guide said, "I am very sorry to have to tell you this, but there is no doctor. There was a man this morning, very sick, but I could not find a doctor for him."

I left Moria feeling angry. Whose fault was this horrible mess? I wanted to find out.

We discovered that we were too late for the shops, as they close early on Saturday, so we went to look at the other camp, Kara Tepe.

The difference was astonishing. First, the entire terrain was covered with nice UNHCR cabins, and it looked as if everyone had a roof over their heads. Some people had little campfires outside their cabins. One man told us he had arrived a couple of hours before and had already registered. He would be boarding a ship to Athens that same day. The lines for registering were much shorter than at Moria, and everything looked very well organized.

Kara Tepe had a proper entrance, with big welcome signs. Nearby there was a stand with a UNHCR worker helping people. I asked her why there was no one welcoming people at Moria. She was interested, and said "please tell me about it," but she didn't know anything about Moria. A woman was sweeping the path. The toilets were clean. There was a sign showing the way to the doctors' tent and saying what hours it was open. I followed it and went to speak to the Médecins sans Frontières spokesman, a dynamic-looking Italian anthropologist. I had to wait a while, since he was speaking to the press.

I said it looked like they were doing a great job at Kara Tepe, but what about Moria? The spokesman said, "Ah, Moria is my favourite camp!" I didn't get this, and asked him to explain. What he meant was that he saw it as a great challenge and was looking forward to tackling the problems there.

"Why hadn't they done so before?" I asked. He had only received permission to start working at Moria two weeks before, he said. They were now busy setting things up. I hoped they would hurry up about it!

We drove back to Molyvos, stopping at the Lidl supermarket on the way. After dinner our neighbours invited us over for a drink. In total we were six women, mostly if not all gay, from the UK, Portugal, New Zealand, Norway, and Holland, all working for Starfish. We stayed up until 1:30 talking politics. Someone asked Heleen what her job was, and she said, a little reluctantly, that she was a judge, responsible for hearing immigration cases, among other things. Anne mused how strange it was being camp manager:

"I am 25, and I ask this ... judge to go and clean the camp!" We reassured her that this was fine, and she was doing a great job.

The others went out for some rare late night fun, to a local bar. We later heard that they had all gone dancing until 5 a.m., but we went to bed. I imagined that many of the unattached volunteers might well be getting together in the late hours, releasing tension and perhaps testing out certain glances exchanged during the day, or signals conveyed by arms that had brushed casually over a gleeful child or a box of shoes.

12. EFTALOU

On our free Sunday we set off from Molyvos
for an hour and a half's walk (at my slow pace)
to the beach at Eftalou, where many of the
refugee boats land. It was at Eftalou that
people would board their first bus, the one
that took them to Oxy. We hiked on the scenic
route up and down through olive groves and I
needed my stick. We recalled the 11 million
olive trees our cab driver had told us about.
First we passed the football field. Refugees
who were rescued by the Greek coastguard
were technically under arrest and they were
brought here after first being registered at the
harbour. They were then taken straight to
Mytilene instead of going to Oxy. But today
the football field was being used for an actual
game of soccer, with thirty men along the
sidelines shouting encouragement: Molyvos
versus nearby Petra? We didn't find out.

As we walked in a slow arc around the hill of Molyvos, we passed a man beating the branches of a tree to harvest olives. We saw a stack of beehives in someone's farmyard. Several dogs came out, wagging their tails in welcome, not barking. There were lots of dogs and cats here, and almost all seemed healthy and well fed. Eventually we arrived on the other side of the hill, and saw the castle from the east.

As we approached Eftalou, we started to meet oncoming groups of refugees who were walking to Oxy instead of waiting for a bus. They were mostly young men. We waved and said "Welcome!" and they smiled cheerfully and said "Hello!" in return. This was probably the best part of their journey. They were relieved to have survived the brief but treacherous crossing in a flimsy dinghy, and were exhilarated to be safe, away from war and devastation and finally in Europe. They had met kind, welcoming people at Eftalou and would meet more at Oxy. Life was good! Then they would go to Mytilene, and from then on, for many of them, things would rapidly go downhill. Again and again I would notice that the young men looked excited, full of energy, while the women, especially the women with children, and older men with families, looked drained, apprehensive, and brittle.

When we got to the beach, we started to see the expected mounds of orange life jackets. Also an occasional punctured black dinghy at the waterline, sprawled and shifting in the tide like a lazy stingray. Refugee families sat around on mats on the beach, almost as if they were having a picnic. Children played, their parents looked a little dazed. There was no bus yet.

We walked towards the hot springs of Eftalou, a popular tourist spot, though it seemed to be closed now. A Scottish photographer pulled up, parked at the side of the path to the springs, and leapt out to take pictures of the refugees. Then along came a Slovenian man who wanted to serve tea to people waiting for the bus. A Starfish volunteer was explaining that it was not sensible to serve tea too close to the bus. So the Slovenian went off to set up his tea tent behind the Scottish photographer's car. (Later in the day we saw an irritable message in our WhatsApp group asking if anyone knew who had set up a tent on the path to the springs without asking permission from the local authorities).

We went to see the arts and crafts workshop of Eric and Philippa Kempson. Eric creates extraordinary sculptures from olive wood, which is notoriously hard wood – most people consider it almost impossible to carve – and Philippa makes olive-wood and gemstone necklaces and earrings. At the entrance to the workshop stands a magnificent model village, complete with hilltop church, carved from a single trunk of an olive tree, the paths and little houses following the natural caprices of the wood. Stunningly beautiful.

At the side of the house in a roofed-over storage area are shelves stacked high with plastic boxes. These boxes do not contain art materials. They are marked "children's socks," "men's trousers," "women's underwear" etc. Ever since the refugees started arriving at Eftalou in large numbers, towards the end of 2014, Eric and his wife have helped them to disembark on the rocky beach in safety. Soon Eric was getting up early every day and scanning the horizon with a pair of binoculars, warning the Greek coastguard if a boat was in trouble.

After several months Eric was joined by groups of volunteers, in particular the Dutch Boat Refugee Foundation, a team that includes doctors, who had their own large tent on the beach (*with* permission from the authorities), and the Norwegian outfit Drop in the Ocean (who call themselves "drops"). A couple of Starfish people would also provide assistance and arrange for supplies from Molyvos when needed. There were – and still are – often numerous other people on the beach, sometimes helpful, sometimes less so. The press, too, ranges from journalists who put down their cameras to help someone in distress to the occasional photographer who pushes an aid worker out of the way to get a better picture of someone struggling ashore.

There was a discussion on our Facebook page about the imbalance in numbers: there were often too many people helping on the beach and too few at the camps. Although most people who come here are very well-intentioned, some are eager for the adrenaline rush of welcoming a boat arrival, and less willing to hand out sandwiches, sort clothes, or pick up rubbish.

We spoke to the people at the Dutch Boat Refugee Foundation tent, newly arrived and still fresh – so different from the despondent doctor on their team who had gone home the previous week. He had written movingly on the organization's Facebook page about his feelings of despair after trying to reanimate children who had spent too long in the water after the terrible shipwreck of 28 October.

I saw a fishing boat out at sea, and thought of the Greek fishermen who were going out every day and scarcely had time to fish any more. They had saved hundreds of lives. They had also fished up many dead bodies. Who would give them counselling, aftercare? Someone had suggested on the Lesvos volunteers' website that a fund should be set up to help them. But someone else soon replied that they would be too proud to accept. They would certainly refuse, a third voice chimed in, since it might create the appearance that they had a financial interest in saving lives. Furthermore, it would draw a strange distinction between them and the many other locals who were making sacrifices to help the refugees. It was complicated. Everything here was complicated. At that moment, this felt like the most complicated patch of land in the world.

13. VOLUNTEER MEETING

That evening we had a meeting for all Starfish volunteers at an upstairs gallery at the harbour. When we had first arrived in Molyvos, the organization had been severely overstretched, with just twenty-five people to cover all the shifts. Now, with an influx of new people drawn in part by reports of the disastrous shipwreck of 28 October, the entire room was full. We had almost seventy people, not counting those who were on shift. Numbers varied wildly, since some people stayed for only a few days. (At that time, Starfish was willing to accept people who wanted to help for a short period of time; they could always clean up, make sandwiches, or sort clothes. A couple of weeks after this meeting, however, it was decided that new Starfish volunteers would in future have to sign up for a minimum of a month, to guarantee continuity.)

People sat around on the floor, leaning against the wall. The Oxy dog, Kanella (Cinammon), walked back and forth before deciding at whose feet she wanted to snuggle up. It was wonderful to see that we now had a full staff and would be able to open the children's tent!

During a brief introduction round each person gave their name and home country: Germany, the Netherlands, Britain, Greece, Denmark, Norway, Sweden, Ireland, Spain, Portugal, France, Switzerland, Cyprus, Romania, the United States, Canada, Ecuador, New Zealand, Australia. And this was just a single evening. When we had gone all the way around the room, there was a spontaneous round of applause for this wonderful list of countries, this world!

We had heard that after our regular agenda, some UNHCR representatives would be talking to us about security. In the early part of the meeting, Melinda, leader of the Starfish volunteer organization, expertly handled a range of agenda points. She urged us to drive safely and informed us of the public address system that she had ordered to improve information. She touched on the problem of some refugees at Oxy who avoided the toilets and went up the hill behind the camp instead, resulting in a sanitation problem in the event of rain. The toilets were clean, so people suggested a variety of other reasons. A clean-up was arranged, along with design improvements to the toilets. Then Trace talked about shifts and the importance of arriving on time. She discussed the importance of good internal communication and set up a group to discuss ways of improving it.

One of the UNHCR representatives started on his talk about good practices to prevent any aggression arising at Oxy. We seldom encountered any aggression at Oxy, but one never knew what might arise. Disappointingly, it soon became clear that he was merely going to take us through his standard powerpoint presentation. He told us things we already knew and advised us to do things we already did: give people information, issue tickets, be fair, explain why some people are being prioritized, create safe lines, and so on. People started drifting away, some in mind, others in body.

One of the camp managers, Omar, had a question about a specific issue he had faced. He had collected a family with two small children from the beach and brought them to Oxy. A doctor in attendance on the beach had told Omar that he had sedated the husband because he was a heroin addict. The doctor warned that when the man came round, it was possible that he might be very aggressive to his family, to others, or to himself. Omar wanted to know what he should have done, what is permissible, in such a situation. Should he tie up a person who might constitute a threat? Was that not a human rights issue? Suppose the man died, could he be liable?

The UNHCR representative said: "If there is violence, first protect yourself and others, take care of the vulnerable. Get the security guard. Then call the police." This was not very helpful. One of our security guards was at the meeting. Although there are a few policemen who live in Molyvos, he explained, the local police station has been closed due to financial cuts. The nearest one is at Kalloni, some thirty minutes' drive away.

"How about the police at Mytilene?" the UNHCR man wanted to know. That is over an hour's drive away. Eventually the UNHCR man said Omar would have been justified in tying the man up, but the other questions remained unanswered. In this specific case the situation had resolved itself reasonably well. When the man had woken up he had merely wept and needed comforting.

During the discussion of measures to deal with security issues, there was an odd clash.

"I have just heard the word 'violence' mentioned seven times, but we have no violence at Oxy, the refugees are very peaceful!" a woman said, in clear irritation. A few others murmured agreement. They disliked talk of security and violence, and thought it unnecessary. Others thought it obvious that a security protocol needed to be in place, however rare the incidents might be. The bottom line was that if something happened, we needed to solve it ourselves.

14. BUS LOADING
AND FARSI PHRASES

On Monday I was assigned to bus loading. I was a bit nervous, since I hadn't done this before. The bus loading area at Oxy was well arranged, cordoned off and divided into lines, with one volunteer at each end of the line. The ropes between the lines were covered with wet clothes that refugees had hung there to dry.

A Londoner called Suleman explained the system to me, since he had done this shift several times before. I warmed to Suleman straight away and looked forward to getting to know him better. He showed me around the bus loading area. Each line had a board at the entrance to which tickets were clipped, with an arrow indicating the order in which buses would load: first the orange ticket with the circle, then the blue one with a star, and so on. There were separate lines and boards for the "Syrian" buses going to Kara Tepe and the "non-Syrian" buses going to Moria. The ticket tent issued fifty tickets for each bus; small children were not given tickets since they were expected to sit on their parents' laps.

The most important thing here, aside from keeping order, was to make sure that families were not split up. This could be difficult in the case of very large families.

A young man from Afghanistan kept coming up to us. He seemed very uneasy. First he said he was 17. Half an hour later he was 21. Then he asked if it was better to be 17 or 21. Was it an advantage to be a minor? We told him not to lie, that the authorities had ways of testing a person's age. He was also worried about fingerprinting. Perhaps he had heard that if a person is fingerprinted in Bulgaria, he can be sent back there. That is possible, but we assured him that if he was fingerprinted in Greece, he would not be sent back to Greece. That has been true for years now.

A bus brought in some wet people from the beach about an hour later, but after that we heard that the flow of boats appeared to have stopped. This interruption did not seem to be related to the weather, which was good. Someone suggested that there might be a political reason: the Turkish president Erdogan was visiting the coast, which meant a heightened police presence. When this happened, the boat mafia would lie low until the police had gone. But this was just a rumour, a guess.

I took the opportunity to try to improve my

Farsi. I had already learned a few useful things in Arabic, such as "only for children!" and "stand in one line!" but my Farsi was useless. Many of the Afghan refugees only understand Dari, which is a variant of Farsi. So far I only knew that milk was *shir*, and that was really not good enough. So I googled to find essential phrases in Farsi, which is called "Persian" on most basic language sites. I found a site with essential phrases like "Happy Valentine's Day!" and "When are you coming back?" Oh, that was part 5 of essential phrases. So I looked for part 1.

Ah, Part 1 of Essential Phrases in Persian.

"You are big!"

"The light wraps you."

"A red rose is like a hot kiss."

"I want to do to you what the spring does to the cherry tree."

By then it was 7 p.m. Boats had started arriving again, and we knew that we would soon be greeting new arrivals. I gave up my efforts in Farsi for the day and opened up the food tent.

15. SOUP AND SONG

I found myself working at the food tent yet again. Trace had evidently decided that this was the best place for me. Someone had fixed the bendy door to the hut nicely with duct tape. I was working with a young Swede, who explained that the Swedes had a saying: "If it moves and you don't want it to move, use duct tape. If it doesn't move, and you want it to move, use WD40." So Swedish people will sometimes give each other presents consisting of a package with a roll of duct tape, a can of WD40, and a bottle of wine: guaranteed to solve all problems. This is surely the mentality that produced Ikea.

After a couple of hours the influx of boats stopped again, and we went outside to help clean up. Because of the slowdown, the IRC told us they would not be sending any more buses that day. Our camp manager, Omar, went off on his scooter to Eftalou to reconnoitre boat arrivals and to convince the IRC to send more buses if needed.

During the clean-up operation, discarded camp beds turned up, three of them lying at odd angles in the cliffs on the other side of the road. They were brought back and piled up outside the main tent. Most refugees spending the night at Oxy would have to sleep on thin mats on the ground, with just a blanket. Distributing blankets was less simple than it sounds: if we were not careful, the supply ran low because people took too many. Once we found a woman using two as a pillow, two to lie on, and four more to keep warm.

Someone handed out the camp beds to refugees who seemed to need them. One man came up and was given one. Then a new volunteer, a rather forceful young woman called Lourdes, or Lou, said "No! They are only for people who are sick!" and took it away from him. He got angry, saying he hadn't slept for three days and was exhausted. I did not understand why Lou thought it was a good idea to intervene.

Someone decided it would be nice to make coffee, and set up a little butane camp gas burner. Someone else pointed out that it was not terribly safe right next to the big UNHCR tent where most people sleep. I began to hope that Omar would soon return from Eftalou.

I watched the huge crane that was lowering a new block of (Dutch!) toilets, donated by the charitable organization Samaritans Purse. Then Omar came back, having successfully persuaded the IRC to resume sending buses; more boats were on the way. As darkness fell, people started arriving from the beaches.

Just as we were getting ready to serve the new group of refugees, a van belonging to the Zahra Trust, one of the many charitable organizations that had come to help, pulled up with a huge cauldron of hot lentil and potato soup to be distributed from the food tent. This was a bit tricky, especially at the point when two or three flimsy plastic plates of hot soup had to be handed out through the window across the piles of sandwiches. There were still two of us in the food tent, but suddenly Lou came in and without any consultation started distributing the soup. I felt a little irritated; she had not been assigned to the food tent, and what was she doing? But then I watched her as she took the plates of soup from the Zahra people who were crouching on the floor to ladle it onto the plates, and handed the correct number of plates to people without spilling anything. The fact was, she was doing an excellent job, and every plate of soup came with a lovely smile. So I took the tickets and did sandwiches and water while she did soup and fruit. My Swedish colleague kept the crates filled. It worked very well.

When the soup ran low, and things became less hectic, there was time for Lou and me to become better acquainted. Lou was a vivacious and intense individual. She was on something of a "high" after having recently defended her PhD thesis. She talked a little about her fascinating development work in Haiti. We parted on very friendly terms. I was relieved that I had suppressed my initial irritation, but not quite ready to accept that my irritation had been out of order in the first place.

A few days later I would feel perplexed by my initial reaction to Lou. I grew to feel very affectionate towards her, and admired the warm dedication with which she did her work. What initially struck me as bossiness was just eagerness, enthusiasm. In that sense, I thought, she was not unlike me. When we had enough volunteers to reopen the children's tent, she devoted herself to entertaining and taking care of the youngest refugees for hours on end. She encouraged them to make drawings. One of them, made by a child of eight or nine years old, depicted a boat with several people floundering in the sea.

I remember one day in which Lou went around with a hand puppet, intending to make the children laugh. Then one of the children looked frightened, and she realized that it was a pig puppet – not such a comical sight for little children from Islamic cultures. She quickly switched to a bear instead.

That first soup evening ended on a magical note. Out of the darkness came a melodious sound we had not heard before at Oxy. A group of refugees were singing songs, with one standing on a crate in the middle. It was wonderful to hear this chorus of plaintive male voices in the night air. Someone was filming them, and I went to see who it was. It turned out to be the award-winning filmmaker Hamy Ramezan, himself an Iranian refugee, who now lives in Finland. At the end of my shift I went over and spoke to him. He was making a documentary, following groups of refugees from the beginning of their European journey in Greece right through the Balkans into Germany. The film will hopefully feature at the 2016 documentary festival IDFA in the Netherlands. I asked where the singing refugees came from. He said that he had initially thought they were Afghan, since they sang in an unfamiliar dialect, but in fact they were Iranian. What were they singing about? They were singing about the love they felt for their country, and how it felt to be so far from home.

16. NO SHOPPING!

I was assigned to the clothes tent the next day, not the most popular of jobs, and tried to put a brave face on it. All the tasks have to be shared, it's only right. And when I grumbled to Heleen that I can't tell a T-shirt from a pair of leggings, she said it was like a man saying he couldn't boil an egg. So anyway, clothes tent. People who had been here in the summer explained that the area had been improved enormously. The men's clothes were now in a separate tent from those for women and children and there was lighting. In short, we had a marvellously modernized facility.

The clothes tent for women and children was another plastic hut like the food tent. Against all the walls were cardboard boxes brimming with donated items.

A group of women and children, fresh from the beach, pressed around the entrance to the hut, exactly like people inspecting a stall at the Monday morning market on Westerstraat in Amsterdam. Pantalons, pantalons! If people asked for trousers, the drill was to bend down and feel their legs, since we only gave trousers to people who were wet above the knees. Almost all boat refugees get wet below the knees, since they have to clamber out into several inches of water when they reach the beach.

"It will dry!" we would say with mimicry, pointing to the sun and fluffing out our own shirts.

Since the children's clothes were a mix of all sizes from toddlers to teenagers, and the shoes were jumbled and often unpaired, meeting each person's needs was not easy. One volunteer would stand outside, try to keep order, and shout needs to one or two people scurrying around inside among the boxes.

"Small boy completely wet!"

"Two underpants!"

"Pregnant lady needs larger trousers!"

(in an undertone) "*Women's period things!*"

"Too big!"

"Too small!"

"Pink?? No, no shopping!"

One of our team went round the camp to retrieve armloads of items that people had accepted from the clothes tent and then decided they didn't want. We put them back in the boxes.

When people crowded in too much, we shouted "Saaf wahed," "saaf wahed!" which means "one line!" At one point we were getting mobbed a bit, and I called on the app for backup. A few minutes later, camp manager Anne arrived, hauling one of the sturdy tables that a carpenter volunteer had made a couple of days ago. She placed it in front of the entrance to create a barrier.

First we marvelled at the wonderful new table, and tried to find a way of getting round it ourselves. Then we decided it didn't really work, since even the person outside couldn't easily reach the women to feel their trousers.

Ellen, an energetic drama graduate who had taken the shift before us and who had been here over the summer, had introduced a system of wall signs explaining what was where, and asked us to keep everything in the right place. At some point she came back, having stayed at Oxy after her shift, and told us about her plans to completely overhaul the clothes tent with a neat shelving system, so that it would soon be everyone's favourite job. Later, when the night shift arrived and I explained about Ellen's plans, one woman shook her head and said it was a terrible idea. "With clothes, shelves are bad" she pronounced flatly. "They must be folded all the time, all the time, all the time. Boxes are much better." I wondered how this dispute would be resolved.

I found a nice pair of shoes for a woman and handed them over. They looked quite new. But she was unhappy. What was the problem? Oh, two right shoes. Sorry! We laughed a bit, until I realized that some less alert person was now going around wearing two left shoes. Someone more experienced arrived and asked, "What are you doing? We don't give shoes unless people have no shoes at all. The shoes will dry. Give dry socks, and plastic bags in between the socks and the shoes."

"What plastic bags?" I said. And then it struck me why we were always running out of plastic bags at the food tent.

I managed to find a good warm coat for a very cold woman. She strung together a lot of Arabic sentences, drawing a circle in the air around the clothes tent, then pressed her hand to her heart and smiled at me so sweetly. I didn't understand a word she said, but I understood completely that she was saying: "I am so grateful, you are all so kind!"

17. HARBOUR DUTY

The next morning I decided to enjoy the sunshine and walked into the village. On the road I met Starfish volunteer Brian, a former teacher, who was coming back from shopping. He and his wife had been for a cruise in the summer and their ship had encountered a refugee boat in trouble. The captain turned the cruise ship back to provide assistance. Although the general mood on board was one of sympathy, Brian had been appalled by some of the comments made by fellow passengers, many of whom were annoyed by the unanticipated delay. Someone had said,

"Oh, they're probably terrorists, why don't we just leave them there!"

But the people who made Brian really lose his temper were those who were delighted with the opportunity to take photos, especially when more refugee boats started appearing around them.

"Now we can show that we saw them!" they enthused.

After returning home, Brian had felt restless and decided he simply couldn't stand to watch the images on TV any more. He had to help, and fortunately his wife encouraged him to come. Many of the volunteers who work on Lesvos have similar stories, of suddenly realizing it was not necessary for them to stay at home, read, and watch. Instead, they could come and help. They had contacted Starfish or another volunteer organization, paid for their own transport and accommodation if they could afford to, got sponsoring if they couldn't, and joined the relief effort. A large proportion of the help provided to the thousands of refugees who arrive here relies on volunteers who have made that decision.

Then I met three Americans who said they were running the operation at Skala Sikamineas, further east along the coast from Eftalou, where there was a camp similar to Oxy. I looked forward to going there to see how they did things.

Heleen and I had the afternoon shift: we were assigned to harbour duty and sandwiches. On the way to the harbour we encountered a Dutch media man arranging his broadcast about the refugee situation with someone on the phone. I walked two paces behind him, hoping to find out what outfit he was with, but my hovering started looking like stalking and I had to give up.

Our German colleague "Ginsberg" made hundreds of sandwiches, and I sat at the harbour on call in case a boat was brought in by the coastguard. It was our task to register the refugees brought to the harbour by the Greek authorities (since they would be technically "under arrest") and take them to the football field, from which a bus would take them straight to Mytilene instead of to Oxy.

I sat with the witty, earnest American doctor Peter and an incoherent though sporadically razor-sharp Irishman who drank and smoked non-stop all day. Our absurd chatter spiralled into mad ranting about politics and I was again reminded of my hippie days at the Melkweg in the 1970s. I did not drink, though, mindful that I was on duty.

At 8 pm we got a call that two boats were on their way. I put my rucksack upstairs in the office at Captain's Table and got ready to do my first registration. Then I realized I had left my head-lamp upstairs and went to get it, since I would be sitting on the jetty with my registration forms in the pitch dark.

When the coastguard finally arrived, there were only eight men from the refugee boats. This would be an easy initiation into registration, I thought. First, ask if one of the refugees speaks a little English. (Luckily, someone did.) Then register each man by his first and last names, father's name, mother's name, nationality, sex, and date of birth. First man: all plain sailing, until we got to date of birth. Birth? I tried several approaches: "When you were born ... when your life began ... you were a baby ... Beginning of life ... Birthday..."

"Twenty-seven" said the "interpreter," pointing to the man I was trying to register. Finally a fellow Starfish pointed out that these men, who were all Afghan, used a different calendar and had no idea of their birth year in our calendar. Stupid of me not to have thought of that. After that we managed to get months, days and age, and calculated the year on that basis.

All the men were terribly hungry and exhausted, having waited for days in the woods in Turkey for the moment they could board a boat. They had not slept for three days. We gave them dry clothes, a little food, and then started arranging for one man with a painful tooth to see a dentist.

I took the registration form to the port police, where three officers sat at their desks. I handed over the form with the eight names.

"Take them to Oxy," said the officer.

"But they were brought in by the coastguard," I said, puzzled.

"Oxy, Oxy," said the officer. "I will tell Melinda." And he phoned Melinda at Captain's Table, two doors away.

I went back to Captain's Table and said to Melinda, "they say the men have to go to Oxy."

"I know," she said, "it's not right, but ...."

We eventually found a volunteer who had a car big enough to take all eight men, and they were taken to Oxy for their first night's sleep in Europe.

18. FRIDAY THE 13TH

It's usually a joke, Friday the 13th. And for much of this day, it still was.

There had been a definite decline in boat numbers over the previous few days, in spite of the beautiful, calm weather. The night before we had heard rumours that one of the major smugglers in Turkey had been caught, leading to one of the biggest boat operations being wound up (or more likely temporarily suspended). We also heard that the imports of rubber dinghies from China had been delayed or stopped altogether. People would be waiting even longer in the woods in Turkey, often without eating or sleeping, before they were summoned to board a boat.

Perhaps this was partly why a larger, wooden boat arrived at Eftalou that morning, with 300 people on board. Fortunately, everyone was able to disembark safely. You would not want to depend on the life jackets that are sold along the Turkish coast. Some are sold very cheaply and are full of straw. Others are more expensive, but many of these too (according to someone involved in testing them) are porous and will not keep a person afloat for very long.

A Canadian reporter arrived at Oxy, looked at the big UNHCR tent and concluded, "Ah, so this camp is obviously run by the UNHCR!" Heleen put him straight, explaining that Oxy was run by Starfish, a volunteer organization. The UNHCR provided the tent and gave us excellent warm blankets when we called for them, but all the people working here were volunteers who were funding their own travel and accommodation. Likewise, all the food, clothing and medical services were also donated and dispensed by volunteers. The journalist, who hadn't heard of Captain's Table or Starfish, set off to Molyvos to get better informed.

Earlier that day, a UNHCR person had arrived at the camp to take a look, and asked why Melinda had called for blankets. Heleen said she didn't know, but that there was a constant need for them. The man got out his mobile and called Melinda to find out. The thing about blankets (there was a thing about everything here) was that when people left Oxy on buses in the cold evening air, they might well want to take their blankets with them. Some said the UNHCR blankets should stay at Oxy, but few would want to ask a cold refugee to give back their blanket when they were going to inhospitable Moria, where they would probably have to sleep in the open air. Later we were told that all refugees must take their blankets with them on the bus, and that recycling them was unhygienic and forbidden.

The Zahra Trust brought individual rice-based meals, and soon the food line stretched down to the road. Some people appeared to be going back to the ticket tent and getting food tickets again and again. The thing about tickets was that some people thought we should not keep handing out food to a refugee we had definitely seen several times before, while others thought that since many of the refugees would be going to Moria, where they might go hungry for days (since at Moria, food depended at that time on random distribution by volunteer groups, without any central coordination), we should feed them up at Oxy and help to build up their strength.

Eventually everyone was fed, and for a while there were no more arrivals. A small group of women, all graduates and politically savvy, gathered spontaneously in the food tent: British, Dutch, Greek, and Spanish. Lou, who had become a friend, has a doctorate in environmental science and comes from Catalonia. She gave us a brief account of social tensions caused by the polarized attitudes to Catalan independence. A woman from Athens discussed the missteps taken by the governing Syriza party and the disappointment among many of its supporters. We reflected on the tendency towards polarization in so many European countries.

The mood lightened as our hilarious Greek security guard appeared at the food window with his immaculate, Elvis Presley appearance and non-stop jokes, all of them unfortunately unrepeatable. He did a tremendous dance routine to illustrate the samba that had been enthusiastically taken up by a fellow villager who had become bored with martial arts. He will undoubtedly make it big in stand-up comedy one day. Why was his hair so carefully coiffed? someone enquired. He said he had decided to spend more time on it after he had been taken for a refugee two days running and directed to the hut where he could get a ticket for food.

At the end of the day, the horrifying news came in of the terrorist attacks in Paris, and Friday the 13th acquired a sinister quality, a day we would never forget. Someone offered condolences to our French volunteers in the WhatsApp group. Someone else cautioned that it might be wise to be extra vigilant in the days to come in case of possible activity by the rightwing groups on the island. But aside from that, everything went on as before. We looked around at the people huddled under their blankets, and recalled that terror, senseless violence, was precisely what they were fleeing from.

19. SKALA SIKAMINEAS

On our free Saturday, Heleen and I set off to Skala Sikamineas, half an hour's drive away, to see how the aid effort was organized there. We hummed and hawed about which road to take. Anne had urged us to take the dirt road along the coast since that is the most travelled path and provides the most interesting experience. But we didn't dare; technically it was "off road" and our car rental firm had explicitly forbidden off-road driving.

Even following the bigger road with its glorious views we got lost, but eventually we arrived on the beach at Skala Sikamineas, another picturesque little harbour full of inviting restaurants. Before lunch I went off to see how the local operation worked. For some reason, eighteen little dinghies had set off almost simultaneously from Turkey to Lesvos earlier that afternoon, forming a ragged line across the sea. I accosted an UNHCR worker who seemed to be taking stock and asked her how many people there were in each boat: as many as fifty? Or sixty, she said. So there was plenty of activity going on at the food and clothes stalls set up behind the beach.

This camp was smaller than Oxy and everything seemed condensed. But Skala Sikamineas had the services of a remarkable Malaysian volunteer chef, Rayyan Haries, who (as depicted on Facebook) wore a hi-vis vest inscribed #askmeforfood and "tea, soup and refugee." He made sweet black tea and a huge tureen of soup every day. Unfortunately I didn't see him, as he was off buying ingredients. He funded his cooking by getting up at 5 a.m. and continuing his full-time work as a digital strategist before getting down to cooking.

Two fellow Starfish joined us for lunch, an English and a Dutch woman. They ordered vast quantities of food, feeling that they deserved it, since they had had a near-death experience. It seems that they had taken the dirt road and had been forced off the road by a truck that was travelling much too fast and did not stop when they screeched to a halt with one wheel hanging over the inside ditch. Fortunately some locals soon came by and lifted the car back onto the road. Hearing this story, we were glad of our cowardice.

20. PETRA

Although I had Sunday off, I wasted it watching the news over and over again, as I always do, obsessively, when the world shudders a little. But did the world shudder any more on that Friday than it did on Thursday? Facebook was suddenly full of people complaining that all this revulsion about the events in Paris, compared to near-silence about a terrible bombing in Beirut the day before, showed our callous Eurocentrism, if not racism. On the one hand this felt so ridiculous that it hardly needed a response: certainly I felt more emotionally connected to Paris than to Beirut, or indeed than to Wellington or Toronto. It's virtually next door, I've been to Paris many times and love it. On the other hand they did have a point, perhaps. "News" is a departure from the norm. When we hear in Europe or America of mass bombings and attacks in certain countries, we are inclined to classify them as routine, even if they aren't.

Sunk in these muddled thoughts, I was pleased to be "rescued" by a plea in our WhatsApp group for someone to go and help in nearby Petra, where the coastguard was bringing in 92 people who would need to be registered for the port police. With my recent experience registering the eight Afghans in Molyvos, I considered myself a veteran of registration and immediately offered to go if "MIP" would come to get me (Heleen had our car at Oxy).

"MIP" is the Starfish car, named affectionately after its registration plate. More importantly, the "MIPs" are the group's drivers. The volunteers who rotate in the MIP shift, which like all the other shifts operate 24 hours a day, work incredibly hard. They buy items from flypapers to plastic bags, search through boxes for clothes, load and unload everything from sandwiches to carpenters' materials, and drive back and forth across the island. One of the core workers at Starfish was the MIP driver Kenny, a guy with an endearing personality who successfully overcame a serious drug problem to become one of the most reliable, conscientious and tireless Starfish volunteers, the person I would be most likely to call if I were in any kind of trouble here. The MIPs also transport other Starfish volunteers when needed, giving rise to a verb, as in "Please mip me up to Oxy." So I was mipped up to Petra.

Two boats had been brought in, one with 26 people on board and one with 66. Once I had figured out how to bypass the wire fence blocking the quayside by going down some steps and along the waterside (without looking down!), I joined the medics and support staff of SCM (the Salaam Cultural Museum, a slightly puzzling name for a group of aid workers) who had come to receive the refugees on the jetty.

The SCM people often worked in the medical tent at Oxy. None of them had any experience with registration, but luckily some of them speak Arabic, and since the first boat consisted entirely of Iraqi Kurds from Mosul, half of whom appeared to belong to a single family, Arabic was essential.

Even with the assistance of my SCM Arabic interpreter, registering the Iraqis took a long time, and when we got to the second, larger group of refugees, who were from Syria – some of them Palestinian – one of the other SCM people starting registering half of the group herself to speed things up. Many of the Syrians had passports, which made things easier. After an hour and a half we had some decidedly odd-looking and inconsistent spellings and a number of people whose birthday consisted only of a year, but we were done. I totted up the totals, 26 in one group, 67 in the other, and gave the registration forms to the port police officer who was waiting for them.

The officer looked at the forms, and his face darkened.

"The number is wrong," he said. "It is wrong, it must be 66 in this group, and look, you have 67."

The SCM woman and I started furiously scanning our sheets to see if we had registered anyone twice. One of the babies, perhaps? Nope, didn't look like it.

"Couldn't the coastguard have possibly – just perhaps – miscounted?" I suggested, as meekly as I could.

"Impossible," said the officer. The coastguard had counted and then the port police officers had counted again. It was 66.

Ten minutes later the problem magically evaporated. "It was 67," announced the officer, as if this had been obvious all along.

Starfish had ordered two UNHCR buses to take these people straight to Mytilene. Once I was sure my help was no longer needed, I went home.

That evening we had another volunteer meeting. Again, some seventy people crowded into the gallery. Melinda told us the sad story of the fire that had broken out the previous evening. A chartered boat (nothing to do with refugees) had caught fire in the harbour, due to some technical malfunction. The fire had spread to a tourist boat belonging to a local man who was dependent on it for his livelihood. The two boats on fire had drifted close to some fishing nets. All this had prompted a handful of malcontents among the locals to accuse Melinda: "It was all her fault. She had brought the refugees here. She was destroying the harbour, destroying the island." The notion that the influx of refugees might in any sense be to blame was particularly ironic, since the presence of a refugee boat had stopped the boats on fire from reaching the nets, thus preventing any damage to them. Later on, someone set up an initiative to help replace the ruined tourist boat.

As Melinda pointed out, "There are people who are for us and work with us, people who are against us, and people who would like to help but are not sure how to do so." Those islanders who object to the relief effort are only a relatively small minority. Like everything else on Lesvos, it is complicated. Some who fear for their livelihood and are frustrated are inclined to blame everything on the refugees and on those who help them, even a chartered boat with a short circuit.

It was announced that volunteers wishing to sign up with Starfish would be asked in future to commit for at least a month. This sent me into a depression: when would I ever be able to come for a whole month again? The fact is, this had been the most extraordinary experience of my life, and I found the thought that I might not be able to return here almost unbearable. Later on, we were relieved to hear that the one-month minimum would not apply to returnees.

21. DARK THOUGHTS

On the Monday after Friday the 13th I worked with a new volunteer from the UK, Guy. We soon fell into an easy distribution of tasks. Guy is one of those people who stores a stock of adages for every situation. For example, when I looked across to the carpenters busying themselves with planks in the big UNHCR tent and said "It's taking a long time to lay that floor," Guy replied philosophically:

"It takes the time it takes. Some things you can't rush. If you want a baby in less than nine months, it doesn't help to have two women! That's a builder's joke," he added.

A man appeared before us, most of his head swathed in bandages, with just one eye and part of the right side of his face uncovered.

"What happened to you?" asked Guy.

"Iran," answered the man. Perhaps he hadn't understood the question. Or perhaps he had.

"You were bombed?" I asked.

"Police," he said. He'd had enough questions, clearly.

Our new neighbours at Nadia's Apartments, American students, were working at the children's tent. They told us about two children from Damascus, in Syria. The three students had had lots of fun playing with the kids, especially with the little girl, who was about eight years old and very cheerful. Both children had severe burn scars all over their bodies and part of their faces. The little girl had stumps instead of fingers. I tried to imagine her future in Germany, where most of the Syrians were heading. Would she be able to get prosthetic fingers? I had never seen prosthetic fingers, as opposed to a prosthetic hand, and started pondering whether they could work.

It was hard to avoid succumbing to occasional waves of darkness, especially after the events in France on Friday. How would they affect the public mood in Europe and the willingness to admit people fleeing from war? I tried to lighten my own mood by watching the young German Florian, who entertained the refugees with his juggling for hours at a stretch. He was getting better every day. But every time I tried to film him he hurled the ball high in the air and then dropped it.

I saw a black rucksack standing all alone in the middle of Oxy. Looking around for someone who might claim it, I was unable to suppress a sense of unease, and stood looking at it, with unwelcome fantasies flitting through my head accompanied by a familiar phrase: "if you see an unattended bag, please alert the authorities." I had an absurd fledgling fear, following the events of Friday the 13th, that some rightwing lunatic might take it into his head to target the camp, to target the refugees. (When I first wrote about this abandoned rucksack in my blog, I did not explain what I was afraid of. I had not thought it necessary, since from where I stood it seemed obvious. But someone reading the blog entry in Amsterdam assumed that I was afraid that some maniac had infiltrated the refugees and planted a bomb. I was so appalled that I immediately edited the entry to clarify what I meant. If anyone thinks that such a thing is remotely possible, all I can say is: please, come and work with refugees yourself, and you will see how ludicrous this is).

I mentioned the rucksack to my fellow Starfish Brian, the former schoolteacher, who boldly went up to it, opened it up, and discovered that the bag was full of wet clothes. I felt a little foolish.

Many people expressed indignation about the reports that one of the Paris terrorists may have passed through the Greek island of Leros on the way to his murderous mission. Almost a million people fleeing from war and mayhem had passed through Greece in 2015. Some minuscule percentage of them may perhaps have been intent on doing harm, just as a tiny percentage of Dutch, French or British people may be intent on doing harm. But terrorists are very unlikely to opt for this route, since those with the money to purchase sophisticated weapons can also afford to buy convincing false passports and plane tickets. Are they likely to hide in the woods for days, undertake a hazardous crossing in a flimsy little rubber dinghy and then tramp across the Balkans if they can simply fly to London or Paris? I believe that I am more likely to pass the occasional person with murder in his heart while taking my dogs to the park in Amsterdam or London than at a refugee camp.

Heleen had made friends with a lovely, intensely warm-hearted Canadian Starfish volunteer named John. He had become depressed when a countryman contacted him to say that if there was an attack in their country, he would blame John. Like the villagers blaming Melinda for the fire on the tourist boat, some people find refugees and those who help them an easy target. They are not much bothered by logic or rational argument.

22. BECAUSE HUMAN

Arrivals were slow, so I left my fellow worker at the food tent and went to learn about tickets. Partly, perhaps, I was pleased to get out of the food tent because twelve boxes of bananas had just been delivered. Our bananas came from Costa Rica, and someone had said casually:

"Oh, just watch out for the spiders."

"Big ones?"

"No, no, not so big. Just SO big," showing me a fist. "But they're not tarantulas or anything, just, oh, Brazilian jumping spiders."

So I found myself feverishly googling spiders and discovered first the Brazilian wandering spider, which turned out to be the most venomous spider on earth and is known for the unearthly little dance it does before killing you. Then I found jumping spiders, of which there are many. These, I was relieved to discover, are not dangerous, despite their off-putting "herky-jerky way of moving."

The ticket tent was where new arrivals went first. One ticket each for food and another for the buses to Mytilene. At that time we were doing yellow tickets with a triangle for the next "Syrian" bus, and purple with a bird for the next "non-Syrian" bus. We issued 50 tickets for each bus, and the colour and symbol indicated the order of departures. Numbers are not functional in this situation, partly because some people are illiterate. So we used colours and pictures instead. The purple tickets were nearly finished and we would soon be needing a new batch. I scrabbled among the remnants in the bag and found a batch of 33 orange tickets with a tortoise. I am not good at drawing, but I did my best, since we only needed another 17 tortoises to have a full pack of 50. Camp manager Omar dropped in and shook his head.

"Please, draw simpler pictures on the tickets!" he groaned. I wanted to explain that the tortoises were not my idea, but he had gone.

For a time I worked with a volunteer who spoke fluent Arabic.

"Where are you from?" we asked a man with a family of four at the window.

"Syria," he said.

After they had moved on, clasping their Syria bus tickets, my partner said,

"They are not from Syria, they are from Iraq. Different dialect." There are indeed many dialects in Arabic, which was sometimes a cause of confusion.

I wondered what would happen to the family, when it was discovered that they were not Syrian. Would they be sent from Kara Tepe, the more pleasant camp, to Moria? I decided I needed to find out. (I did eventually find out, and the answer was that once it became apparent that someone had lied, he or she would be sent to Moria after all. It would simply slow down the registration process.)

At the ticket tent I learned some new Arabic phrases. One of the first things that many people ask when they arrive on the beach is "where am I?" It may seem strange, but some people have fled to Europe with very little idea of its geography. There are those who think they are in Athens, and those who assume they are not so far from Germany. So in case they had not quite assimilated the answer, dazed with relief at surviving the boat trip, we would tell them again:

"You are now here (pointing to Molyvos on a map) on the island of Lesvos."

The Arabic for "the island of Lesvos," I discovered, was "al Jazeera Lesvos," so I pondered the implications: the excellent TV station based in Qatar (the only English-language channel we could receive at our apartment) calls itself "the island" because – as I read when I looked it up later – it is the only independent news network in the Middle East.

I walked around the camp at the end of my shift. Ellen, mistress of the clothes tent for women and children, had been advancing her two grand passions – for signs and shelves. Within the space of two days, she had covered the site with signs to the clothes tent over which she presided, and arranged for a carpenter volunteer to cover all the walls with shelves. I had to admit, it looked pretty damn impressive in there. And no one was likely to ever lose their way to the women's clothes tent again.

Outside the UNHCR tent I met an elderly man, travelling alone, who was deciding where to go. He had been living in Syria, but his status was that of a Palestinian refugee. He looked weary. There was a kind of permanent disbelief in his eyes. He said,

"Come, come and see!" I followed him over to his little rucksack, from which he extracted his Syrian "passport," which stated on the front: "Travel document for Palestinian Refugees." This man was perhaps about my age. I wondered how long he had been a refugee. Since 1976? Since 1967? Could he have been born in a refugee camp?

"Holland?" he suggested, when I asked where he was going. He had a son in Sweden, but thought he would be able to bring his wife over sooner if he settled in Holland.

"It might take a long time in Holland too," I said sadly, and then immediately regretted it.

"Before, Holland was good. Now not so good?" he asked, with a defeated air. Then something happened and the man disappeared, perhaps towards the bus line. I was angry with myself. We are cautioned not to make any comparative suggestions to refugees. We may be wrong, and events on the ground move fast, sometimes from one week to the next. Later I tried to find the man again, wanting to undo the impression I had inadvertently given. I recalled the time, decades earlier, when someone had said to me quite casually, "Why not try Amsterdam?" I followed his advice, and have spent the rest of my life there.

This exchange made me think about the fact that I was rarely relating on a personal level to individual refugees. I was helping the group as a whole, but my one-to-one interaction was mostly with other volunteers. This was partly because we were running a transit camp, and my work was mostly in the food tent, handing out sandwiches. But partly also, it was a protective mechanism. I felt the contrast between this man's life and my own privileged existence so acutely at that moment. It was painful, and it paralyzed me. I was also afraid of saying the wrong thing. Offering sympathy without advice is not my strong suit.

In the evening Heleen and I went to buy some supplies at a local shop and talked to the owner.

"We are happy that you are here," he said, "Because you help."

I wondered if his own ancestors were refugees. Lesvos has a history of forced migration. In 1922–1923, thousands of Greeks fled from the Ottoman Empire in boats after what the Greeks call "the Asia Minor Catastrophe," part of what is known as the "Greek genocide." Many settled on nearby Lesvos; over half of the island's population of just 89,000 descend from those refugees. This undoubtedly helps to explain why, despite the locals' concern for their future, the majority feel a sense of empathy with the refugees' plight that is horribly lacking in certain other parts of Europe.

Many refugees passed this shop on their way from the beach to Oxy. Once, the owner told us, a little refugee girl, maybe nine years old, had been sitting on the path outside his shop and suddenly keeled over. She was carrying a very heavy rucksack, he said, and two heavy bags. The shopkeeper went outside, picked her up and dusted her off. Then he watched in consternation when the family got up and set off again. He dashed after them, took the heavy rucksack off the girl's back and placed it on her father's back. After telling us this story, the shopkeeper sighed and then fell silent.

"You help because the people of Lesvos too know what it is to be refugees," I suggested.

"No," he said shortly. "We help because human."

23. TRANSFORMATION

I took up my usual post in the food tent, which was oddly occupied by a bicycle that I had to stretch over constantly to get to the bottles of water. I texted a terse message asking the bike's owner to take it away.

I had time to go out for a chat, and introduced myself to Heleen's friend John, who was working on the shift we called "flexible" around the grounds. That meant cleaning up and helping wherever the need arose.

"Hi! I'm John! From Canada!" he said.

"I know!" I said.

"How did you know?" he asked.

"Because it says 'John from Canada' in big letters on your hi-vis vest," I answered, and we laughed. We soon became good friends. John had taken a special interest in a little boy called Gazi and his family, and was anxiously hoping that they would be able to travel to Germany without mishap. (This would be one of our happiest stories, since a month later we heard that Gazi and his family were safe in Germany, and John was making plans to go and visit them there.)

After a couple of busy hours, we were briefly twiddling our thumbs when two ginormous trailer trucks turned up, taking up much of the space where the IRC buses usually parked. Special gifts for Oxy! One of the trailer trucks was a huge mobile kitchen, and the other was crammed with items ranging from a massive generator, a defibrillator and a festival-standard public address system to wet suits and diving shoes for rescue workers, thousands of blankets and ponchos, and cooking equipment. The PA system would make it possible to inform people in English, Arabic and Farsi of crucial information such as imminent bus departures and mealtimes. The convoy and its contents were arranged and transported by a passionate group of determined people from the Netherlands. Not for the first time, I felt proud to be Dutch!

One of the leading lights behind this great project was the singer Laura Jansen, who knew my musician daughter Tessa Rose Jackson. She arrived with the convoy, and we took a celebratory photo of the two of us together.

The cook André told us the mobile kitchen's history. A couple of months earlier, refugees moving north through Europe who arrived at the station at the border between Serbia and Croatia had to tramp about a mile, often in the dark and sometimes in pouring rain, to get to the bus stop in Croatia where they could continue their journey. So various helpful people had set up stalls along the way, making their trek to the bus stop a surreal kind of free shopping mall. As they struggled along with their babies and bags, the people could get dry clothes and shoes, plasters, and medical attention. From the mobile kitchen, which was part of this shopping mall, the people were served a wonderfully nutritious soup prepared by André, himself a Kurdish refugee from Iraq. The kitchen has the capacity to produce 10,000 meals a day, or 1,200 meals an hour. André described his soup to us in loving detail, from the lentil, potato and tomato base (tomatoes being used to avoid the need for water) to the various additions that would make the soup different and interesting every day. We looked forward to tasting it.

Eventually the international volunteers had persuaded the Croatian government to extend the road to the border, so that the refugees would no longer have to walk a mile, but could board a bus straight away. Exit shopping mall. The mobile kitchen was no longer needed in Croatia, so the organizers decided to move it to Lesvos.

Meanwhile, a major winterization project was getting under way at Oxy. We had few refugees, and the weather was still good, so it was essential to get the camp ready before the rain came. A construction worker rumbled into the grounds on a bulldozer and set about levelling the rocky terrain to make room for a second big UNHCR tent to accommodate another 200 people.

The operation included emptying all the "tents," that is, huts, of their contents and moving them to different places. This was particularly sad for Ellen, who had devoted such time and energy to getting wonderful new shelves installed in the women's and children's clothes tent, and now had to watch as they were all dismantled again. To her credit, I did not hear her grumble once. She's one of those tireless people who takes everything in her stride.

Someone later mused about insurance, liability: people on construction sites wear helmets, a fashion item that is seldom seen in Greece. In fact Ellen and Kirsten had skidded out of a bend in the road on their scooter that morning and appeared at the camp with scarred lips, elbows and knees. Luckily no head wounds. I have rarely seen anyone "sissy" enough to wear a helmet on a scooter or a motor bike here. Later that day I saw a Greek couple riding a scooter with their toddler sitting in front on the driver's lap, waving.

As the light waned and an IRC bus rode off with the last refugees, a Dutch volunteer finished setting up the PA system. As we walked over to the car, the speakers were blaring the Monty Python song, "Always look on the bright side of life"!'

On our way home, we passed the elderly Greek cleaner who often sits on a wall at the roadside near our house.

"How are you?" we asked. "*Ola kala?*"

"Better, better", he invariably answered. He had an optimistic cast of mind.

And it was true. Everything was getting better all the time. Soon we would all be eating nutritious soup. Not as soon as we had hoped, however. Someone forgot to apply for the necessary license for the kitchen. Oops.

24. HIGH STANDARDS

While Oxy was being transformed by digging machines and an army of carpenters, electricians and DIY enthusiasts, I was scheduled to do an early shift on harbour duty. If people had been rescued by the coastguard, this involved receiving and taking care of them, registering them, giving them dry clothes, food and water, and walking them up to the football field where the UNHCR bus would come and collect them to take them to Mytilene. If Oxy was busy but no one had been rescued by the coastguard, harbour duty involved going up to the Sandwich Factory and slapping hundreds of pieces of processed cheese onto pieces of processed white bread.

There were no coastguard rescues that day, and we sat at Captain's Table discussing why the flow of boats to the island had dwindled. Some thought there were political reasons: perhaps it was related to Prime Minister Tsipras's visit to Turkey to conduct negotiations on the flow of refugees, since the Turkish coastguard often seemed to acquire better interception resources when there were bigwigs in the area. Perhaps it was the weather: although it was still fine, there was quite a stiff south wind, which might be too much for the dinghies' little engines. They would keep getting blown back to Turkey.

If someone was stupid enough to mutter that there was nothing to do, Kenny would retort with barely suppressed anger that we should be very thankful if there was nothing to do on harbour duty. I knew why.

After the terrible shipwreck of 28 October, when hundreds of people had ended up in the sea, flailing in their frequently useless life jackets, Kenny had been one of those who had leapt down to the harbour to help as lifeless or near-lifeless bodies of children were brought in. This young man, with his light-hearted banter and missing front teeth, had been one of the day's many heroes, cradling and warming limp children, and performing CPR tirelessly for what seemed an impossible time in an attempt to revive one child whose body failed to respond as the father stood shrieking with torment beside them. So Kenny did not want to hear any complaints from people about there being too little to do on harbour duty.

The Norwegian woman who said "so many people come and go" when I had tried to introduce myself could remain silent for hours at a time. Even her text messages were cryptically concise, as in "sitrep sw fridges not to go." She and others had made thousands of sandwiches that morning, and all the fridges at the sandwich factory were full. She was the most over-qualified sandwich maker in the world. She preferred not to go to Oxy since she knew only too well how major agencies work, and her sensibilities were offended by the rather improvised and impromptu way we operated there: she would have said, perhaps, that our procedures were all wrong. Still, Oxy had been praised by so many professionals that I was confident that her standards were a little too rigid.

Heleen swept the quayside, right down to the house of the elderly man living there. He would sometimes open and shut his door again and again in the throes of some indecipherable emotion.

I did very little, and was feeling guilty. Then, suddenly, at 12:30, someone sent us all a five-page memo about what to do on harbour duty, including what to do when you've got nothing to do. Sandwiches, cleaning, and making bus tickets. I said I would make tickets, and texted a query as to which ones I should make. I received an immediate response from the intense young German Lucas, who said he would show me how to make bus tickets when he got off his shift at Oxy. Clearly, it was not a task that could be entrusted to anyone who had not been properly instructed.

So I stayed on after my shift to learn how to make bus tickets. Lucas arrived from Oxy, fetched sheets of coloured cardboard and the paper guillotine from the office upstairs, and arranged everything on one of the outdoor restaurant tables. He demonstrated ticket-cutting with meticulous precision, indicating the marks on the cutter: Take four sheets, mark at 5-cm intervals here, then 7-cm intervals here, then rotate the cardboard 180 degrees, he urged with emphasis, and mark at 5-cm intervals along the other end too. Then put two of the four sheets aside, since each sheet makes 25 tickets and two sheets are exactly 50 tickets, which is one busload. Cut carefully at the marks using the paper guillotine. Lucas explained to me how to make bus tickets in more detail than anyone has ever explained anything to me before.

Once he had finished his lesson, he watched over my shoulder for half an hour while I cut the tickets. Every now and then I looked around, and there he still was, standing and watching to check that I was doing it properly. Eventually he went and sat at a restaurant table up the steps with some other Starfish people, but I was not sure he was not still watching me. I concentrated on making every single ticket exactly 5 by 7 centimetres so as not to violate Lucas's high standards. Once I was disconcerted to find I had missed a ticket, and counted the last pile to make sure that was where it belonged. I did not want to run the risk of having one pack of 49 tickets and another of 51.

I went on cutting until it was dark and then presented Lucas with 12 neat batches of 50 tickets. He gave them a measured approval.

Heleen and I had our last dinner together, since she was going to leave on Friday. We went to the local Women's Cooperative Restaurant, which has terrific food and was one of our favourite haunts. Anne joined us, and over her choriatiki salad she told us the story of her love affair with Maria, the Portuguese nurse who had come to Lesvos on a leave of absence from her contract in Saudi Arabia. Anne related how she had plied Maria with invitations and bottles of wine and Maria had finally succumbed to her charms. Later, when they were going back over the events of the previous few weeks, it turned out that Maria had been attracted to pictures of Anne before she arrived. She had hoped they would get together but was too shy to respond. Now, Anne was returning to Norway while Maria was back in Saudi Arabia.

We thought these two young women well suited to one another. Anne had a very particular approach to being camp manager: she called everyone to meet in the middle of Oxy in a little circle at the beginning of her shift, to check that everyone was there and to discuss any special plans for the day. She was scrupulous about calling people to account if they were late. Sometimes her emphasis on discipline clashed with certain other people's attitudes, giving rise to tension. Maria was the brave soul who saved us at the food tent on the night when we seemed to be threatened by a stampede. She made us close the tent while she and others set up a system of ropes and lines for crowd management. I hoped that Anne and Maria would get back together:

these two young women, both of them clever and gently humorous, with strong characters, made a lovely couple.

25. WINDS OF CHANGE

I drove Heleen to the airport in Mytilene, which is right next to the beach. We were almost there when we came across lines of refugees struggling along the roadside with their bags. Apparently one or more boats had just landed nearby: quite unusual, since most boats land on the northern shores of the island. I bought 20 bottles of water at the airport to hand out on the way back, but by the time I drove back the refugees had all vanished.

I went to Oxy and spent a shift bus loading. This could be quite a stressful job when it was busy, since you had to check that people had the right tickets, separating the "Syrian" tickets from the "non-Syrian" tickets and ensuring that people were not jumping the queue. Although 50 tickets were issued for each bus, it was not an exact science, since small children had to sit on their parents' laps and were not given tickets, and there was always the occasional person who slept through the bus's departure and would need to be rescheduled.

That day, however, there were only a few hundred refugees at Oxy, and so not many buses to load. A more pressing problem developed as some of the young volunteers hammered planks and stood on ladders to span tarpaulins to protect queues from the rain and continue the winterization project; a strong wind had blown up. As the man assigned to the ticket tent was more useful at carpentry than I was, I took over the tickets. It soon became necessary to weigh the tickets, maps and pamphlets down so that they did not all fly away.

I watched the tireless Lucas, the young man who had been such a severe instructor in the realm of ticket-making, as he balanced on a table while attaching horizontal struts to the vertical posts separating our boarding lines, which could then be spanned with canvas to protect people from the rain. In a moment of rest, drinking a bottle of water, I said that he had perhaps had too little faith in my ticket-making ability. It seems ridiculous to me now that I needed to say this, but there you are.

"Ah, but I was right," said Lucas. "Because I saw that you did miss a ticket, and you had to count the whole pile to check!" This really creeped me out. It meant that he had been watching me cutting tickets from his restaurant table for an hour and a half! I couldn't figure Lucas out. Was he over-zealous or simply poking fun at me?

Later, however, as the wind intensified and I battened down the ticket tent, which was temporarily an actual tent as opposed to a hut, one of the struts came loose and the wind threatened to lift the entire tent into the air, perhaps with me hanging beneath it as an elderly Mary Poppins or Winnie-the-Pooh clinging to his balloon. At this point it was Lucas whom I instinctively called for help. His thoroughness and total reliability were exactly what I needed. He immediately rushed over with rope and tools and secured the tent. This sort of thing happened again and again. I would find myself first being put off by someone's behaviour, and soon afterwards admiring their positive qualities. This is not in itself an uncommon event, of course, but here everything was speeded up. We were all nationalities here, and each individual a polychrome world. Each volunteer's story, what led him or her to come here, and what each person had to contribute, was as unique as each refugee's story.

We had an interesting moment of linguistic confusion. Several people insisted that we were going to have a storm, while others said definitely not. It was as if the forecasts were wildly different. Suddenly, I figured out what was going on. When German and Dutch people refer to a storm, they mean a very strong wind – what British people call a gale. But to British and American people, a "storm" is always accompanied by rain. I was quite excited by this discovery, and communicated it to the group. A couple of people shared my linguistic enthusiasm, while others looked blank, as if I was ranting about the merits of different potted plants.

Late that evening, we heard that forty refugees had been rescued by the Greek coastguard and were arriving at Petra, very wet. We received urgent requests on our app to pick them up as quickly as possible, and several people set off in cars to fetch them. About three-quarters of an hour later, the refugees arrived at Oxy, having been given dry clothes and water. Half the group came from Afghanistan and the other half were from Somalia. I was staffing the ticket tent, which was still being attacked by gusts of wind.

First I welcomed a group of Afghans who did not speak a word of English, gave them their bus and food tickets and a pamphlet in Farsi, and showed them the route they would be following as clearly as I could by pointing at the map.

Then came the next group, four Somali men, one of whom did speak English.

"So you are a group of four?"

"Yes. As you see," said the man in rather clipped tones. He appeared to think I was being patronizing, since the four of them were standing there, waiting.

The entire group had had a very narrow escape. One related to a team member that the boat had been sinking fast and they had thought they were going to die.

"The water was up to my neck when we were rescued. We all got out our mobile phones to say goodbye to those at home."

Once the new arrivals had settled in, I stood and watched the camp dog, Kanella, cavorting with her new friend, a dog that had appeared at the camp a couple of days earlier. Then, suddenly, they were no longer cavorting but coupling. Fellow team members looked puzzled, peering through the darkness of the camp to understand what was happening. The dogs were joined and facing in opposite directions, and few team members were familiar with the niceties of dog breeding. I warned them not to try to separate the dogs, sent a photo on the group app, and suggested that someone take Kanella to the vet the next day for a morning-after pill. She was to be sterilized soon. The stray dogs were cared for lovingly by the volunteer teams, and at least one of them had been adopted.

At the end of the day I drove two fellow volunteers home to hotels quite remote from the centre of Molyvos, one of them all the way in Eftalou, several miles away. I was thankful for our wonderful apartment with Nadia. I was brooding about the events of the day and my own responses. Why had the linguistic discovery about the word "storm" stayed in my mind longer than the knowledge that the people who had been rescued at sea and brought to Petra, then to Oxy, had very nearly drowned? Was I blocking off my emotions in some way, as a kind of self-protection? Navigating the winding roads in the darkness, I saw a hairpin bend too late and braked sharply, coming to an abrupt halt at the edge of the cliff.

26. LIBRARY TO LIGHTHOUSE

On 21 November I drove down the road to refuel the car, and got into a discussion with the attendant, a good-looking man in his thirties, about the influx of volunteers. He was irritated by what he took to be my implication that volunteers were good for business.

"Yes we may be making €4,000 more than usual this autumn. But next summer we'll we making losses of ten times that amount – €40,000 for sure!"

He expressed a fear that I heard again and again, that tour operators might suspend their trips to Lesvos. This would cause further hardship on an island already dealing with multiple challenges. Hoteliers, restaurant owners and everyone else who depends on tourism for their livelihood were holding their breath, terrified of what next summer might bring, or not bring. (When I got back to Amsterdam I conducted a mini internet survey of Dutch tour operators, from major companies such as D-Reizen and Neckermann to Greece specialists such as Ross Holidays, and was happy to find that not one had scrapped Lesvos from their catalogues. The UK company Thomas Cook did appear to have suspended it from their list of destinations, however, and I did not research the German companies.)

I walked up into the village, and a man about my age, the owner of a local produce store, accosted me, asking my name and inviting me to sit and chat. We sat down on the steps. Like many villagers, he was full of compassion for the refugees. His only concern was the debris. It is true that on some beaches there may be piles of discarded life jackets and dinghies for a while until they are cleared away. But I remembered how astonished I had been when I arrived on Lesvos at the end of October 2015, when 7,000 refugees a day were arriving on the island, to see that most places were very clean. The local council operates regular rubbish collections and groups of locals and volunteers frequently organize cleaning days.

The shopkeeper remained sombre about the future of the island's tourism, and after we had talked for a while, he voiced an opinion that I encountered several times:

"It is partly because you are here that the refugees come to Lesvos!"

I said that this made no sense, that the refugees were fleeing from war and devastation, that they had been arriving in their thousands before the volunteers descended on the island, and that they frequently had only the vaguest idea of where they were going. It was the Turkish boat mafia that pushed the boat out and pointed the hapless man who had been set at the helm – "That way!" Did the shopkeeper really think that the boat mafia chose destinations on the basis of how likely it was that volunteers would be on hand with water and dry socks? This misconception remains a puzzle to me.

I bade the shopkeeper farewell and carried on up the hill to the village's proud library, which serves the community as a lending library and has an impressive store of historical books. It also has a modernizing influence, helping to introduce users to new technologies, and maintains international ties with summer schools in Canada and Norway. The librarian emphasized his solidarity with the refugees:

"Of course – my grandparents were refugees!" he exclaimed.

I spoke about the grandiose plans I had devised in my head: my ideas for Lesvos to become the centre of recycling for the Aegean – surely all the plastic water bottles, life jackets and rubber dinghies could be reprocessed on a grand scale. The librarian smiled ruefully, and mused on the outboard engines salvaged and stacked up in sheds all over the village without anyone taking the trouble to distinguish ones that could be re-used from those that needed to be thrown away .

Recycling is a funny business in Greece. In Molyvos, all the rubbish is jumbled together. In Mytilene, however, it is separated. In one area, at least, the Greeks have an advanced recycling system. People throughout Greece collect bottle caps, and once they have collected a ton (!) of caps, they present them to a charity, which uses the resulting funds to make wheelchairs for the disabled. Could one not build on such a plan, which is very popular in Greece, to introduce a wider-ranging approach to recycling?

There was in fact plenty of recycling going on, but like many things here it was happening on a small, haphazard scale. A fellow volunteer named Suleman, with whom I had struck up a friendship the week before, had written that a group of Greek men would arrive after each boat arrival, cut out the large plastic sheets, and remove the plywood floors and the outboard engine. The plywood was used to make the sides of animal shelters and the plastic was used to make waterproof roofs.

Meanwhile, others were turning life jackets into baby carriers or mattresses to provide insulation for refugees sleeping on the cold ground.

I also spoke to the librarian of my idea for a museum of migration on Lesvos. Surely this island, with its remarkable history, would be a marvellous place for such a museum? I later heard rumours that material was already being collected for a future museum of migration, but I have not yet read of any firm plans. Before I came to the island I had planned to write letters to the press, hoping that I might be able to encourage locals to develop plans that would help the island to recover from its economic malaise.

The librarian liked the sound of both the recycling and the museum projects, but he said:

"It is always the beginning that is most difficult." He also took a more judicious view of his influence, and mine.

"We are just small people," he said. I felt a good deal smaller than him.

I drove down to the beach overlooked by the nearby lighthouse to meet up with Suleman, my new friend from London. He is a witty, softly-spoken man with a sharply perceptive view of events around him. He had been very active here, helping with new arrivals. He showed me around his section of the beach, with separate tents for women and men to change their clothes. The men's tent had a small plant with pink flowers that struck an incongruous note in the corner. Suleman also introduced me to the volunteers of the Hellas Lifeguard Team, and I decided to try to arrange to talk to their leader the next day.

I had not worked on the beaches. Given my age and my bad hip, I thought I would be better employed elsewhere. Suleman too had been writing about his experience here. Helping on the beaches is an essential part of the work done by volunteers on Lesvos, and involves a much higher level of emotional intensity than handing out sandwiches. I read Suleman's account with interest. I would eventually end up on the beach myself, but not until my very last day. I asked him if I might quote from his blog, and he kindly agreed. Here are some extracts from one day's entry, when he was on beach duty at Eftalou:

"The day was beautiful and when we finished litter picking on the beach, including moving many of the discarded life jackets, we sat on a wall drinking water and looking at the beautiful sea.

You can see Turkey from where we were and we saw a couple of orange dots coming towards us. As they got closer we could see they were boats. Orange life jackets usually means Syrians, as these life vests are the least awful and therefore the most expensive. Black life jackets and car inner tubes are the cheapest and usually worn by the Afghans.

One of the boats landed west of us and one arrived exactly where we had been sitting. Before coming here I had tried to mentally prepare myself for all sorts of horrible stuff, including what it would be like to see dead bodies. But what I had not expected was seeing the sheer joy on about eighty faces in a boat for having safely reached Greece. As soon as they were in earshot, we all started slowly clapping (slowly so as not to scare the refugees into thinking they should not have landed there). The refugees joined in. The Norwegians from the volunteer organization Drop in the Ocean arrived from nowhere like blond dervishes, went into the sea up to their knees, helped the people ashore and then disappeared. Once the refugees were all on the beach, families started hugging and kissing each other. I was absolutely not prepared for this show of pure joy. It was beautiful. One of the Syrian men grabbed the side of my head when the bus arrived, pulled it down and kissed my shiny forehead. Very sweet."

27. LIFESAVERS

On Sunday I had lunch with the British volunteer Diana, one of the good friends I have made here. Such a warm, spontaneous person who radiates positive energy. I am sure we will keep in touch. I have made more friends on Lesvos in this month than in the past several years.

I signed up for a shift at Eftalou. I wanted to go there anyway, to speak to the British artists Eric and Philippa Kempson, who have lived on Lesvos for 16 years. I had bought some medical and other supplies I wanted to leave in their storage area, and I also wanted to buy some of their beautiful products. Before leaving the house I also called Spiros and agreed to meet him at Eftalou to talk about the work of the Greek volunteer lifeguards.

In principle the Eftalou shift means standing by in case of boat arrivals, and helping people to board the bus to Oxy. But there was a strong south wind, so we were not expecting any boats. The engines on the little dinghies cannot cope with a stiff southerly wind, which would simply blow the boats right back to the Turkish coast.

The artist couple live in an atmospheric cottage in secluded surroundings down a path leading away from the beach road, with a little artists' studio and shop. Philippa had visitors, and someone had brought cake. We sat around a table in a rather English way with tea and cake, on a small veranda. The house used to have a spacious veranda, but that is now full of shelves of clothes and other items for the refugees. The couple's entire life has been turned upside down. It was over a year ago that Eric and Philippa and their singer daughter Elleni (artist's name EjK) first started helping people to disembark safely and taking care of them. Getting people off the boats safely is often difficult, since much of the coast is rocky, and those who jump out enthusiastically or get out too quickly can easily sprain an ankle, or worse.

"We didn't choose to destroy our lives," mused Philippa. I asked if "destroy" was not too strong a word. She explained that the tourist trade on which they depend has almost dried up, and they have few customers for their products. I have seen Eric's reaction online, when he is asked why they abandoned their normal lives to spend most of their time helping the refugees. He clearly thinks it's a stupid question.

"Because we're human beings!" he will say

bluntly. People needed care, and the idea of not giving that care would have been unthinkable. Eric and Philippa are also fierce about respecting the refugees' dignity.

Philippa was talking about the difficulties they had faced from some of the locals, and I chimed in that most of the people in Molyvos I had spoken to had been full of compassion, though clearly worried about the future. At that point, Eric came in. Eric is sixty years old and sports an idiosyncratic haircut: pudding bowl in the front, shoulder length at the back. I had to remind myself that it is not Eric but his daughter who is the musician of the family. Hearing my defence of the villagers, he became angry:

"We've been spat at! We've had our tires slashed! We've had death threats!"

I knew about this, having watched several of his regular YouTube videos about the refugee situation. In fact it was perhaps his videos that first made me think of going to Lesvos. Eric and Philippa have reacted heroically to the influx of refugees on their doorstep. They, more than anyone, have given up everything to help. And they have received plenty of abuse for doing so. In Eftalou too, some subscribe to the mysterious doctrine that refugees come to that particular beach because Eric and his wife are there – these days with dozens of volunteers from a variety of groups, including Starfish – to help them off the boats, distribute water and hand out dry socks.

Eric expresses himself forcefully on his videos. He voices his disgust at the way the refugees have been abandoned by the EU and by the national governments. He is indignant when the UNHCR promises to deliver tents and then fails to do so. He is outraged by the behaviour of the occasional aggressive photographer, whom he has seen pushing volunteers out of the way, and even, he remarks on his videos, sometimes steering a boat towards a rockier bit of the beach in order to get more sensational photos. Eric was also appalled by the decision to build a new camp along the dirt road, since this road is treacherous in the winter months and unsuitable for the minibuses that are needed to transport refugees up and down between the camp and the asphalt road.

As for the locals, there are undeniably some people in Molyvos who are hostile to the aid effort. It is my understanding that there are even a couple of Golden Dawn supporters, as there are handfuls of fascists in Amsterdam, London, Paris and everywhere else. Eric emphasizes that it is only a few locals who have been aggressive to him.

My own experience is of course very limited. In a month in Molyvos, although I heard a few unpleasant anecdotes, I did not personally see or hear anyone express hostility to or about the refugees. I did see locals bringing food and clothes to Oxy. As Melinda had said, talking about the situation at our Starfish volunteer meeting:

"There are people who are for us and work with us, people who are against us, and people who would like to help but are not sure how to do so."

Spiros arrived, and I sat down with him on a wall outside. Spiros Mitrisakis is the leader of the Hellas Lifeguard Save and Rescue Volunteer Team. Most of his team normally work as athletics instructors at colleges, but they also work part-time providing first-aid training for volunteers and assisting at major events such as the annual swimming event on Spetses and the annual stand-up paddle race through the length of the Corinth Canal.

Following the coverage of the disastrous shipwreck of 28 October, in which so many lives were lost, Spiros and his wife had assembled a team to work on the beach near the lighthouse at Eftalou on a 24/7 basis. They had been incensed by the callous attitudes to the refugees' plight within the EU. Their volunteer work had soon attracted corporate sponsors, including Aegean Airlines, Lalizas, Blue Star, and WIND Telecoms. There are now twelve Hellas lifeguards in total – besides the other lifeguards on the north coast, like the Spanish NGO Pro-Activa Open Arms – working as volunteers on Lesvos:

"Not just men, also women," added Spiros. "Many women refugees don't like to see a big man holding out his hands to help her off boat, or to hold her baby."

I asked Spiros if it was true, as I had heard, that the Greek coastguard service does not allow them to intervene if they see that a boat is in trouble. He shook his head:

"No, but we must phone first, so the coastguard knows who we are, and that we are competent to help." He related a story about a honeymoon couple who had sailed off in a boat hoping to save people, with the best of intentions but no knowledge of what they were doing.

The team had had some dramatic rescues. At one point they went to assist a boat that had run aground on rocks, and as they were helping the people to disembark, the refugees said, "Wait, where is the other boat, the one that had mostly women and children?" The lifeguards set off on a feverish search. An hour later they finally found the other boat, which had become stranded on another part of the coast, and managed to rescue all on board.

Spiros had thought a lot about how to get people off the boats safely onto a rocky beach. It was not always enough to keep them calm and encourage them to disembark slowly.

"So we made a platform. Look!" and he showed me a picture on his phone. Spiros's men were the proud inventors of a disembarkation jetty made from recycled plywood attached to an upside-down rubber dinghy. This enabled the refugees to step onto the platform and simply walk onto the beach, remaining dry.

"We thought, maybe we put a red carpet on top, for welcome!"

The group's selfless dedication had attracted individual donors as well as corporate sponsors. One man came to watch the team at work for a while and was moved and impressed.

"And he said... He said..." Spiros was briefly unable to speak, and I saw that he was overcome by emotion at the memory of the man's words and his generosity.

"He said he admired so much what we were doing. He helped us with our accommodation so that we could stay here for months!"

Spiros's team-mates called him back to the car; they had to leave. I gripped Spiros's shoulder, and thanked him for taking time to speak to me.

After I left Lesvos, there was an incident on the beach in which a photographer whose behaviour had prompted anger in the past, as Eric's videos have recorded, tried to take pictures of refugee women while they were stripping off their wet clothes and changing in a tent. The Greek volunteer lifeguards were angry, and Spiros told the man to go away. He refused, and photographs show Spiros firmly escorting the photographer back to his car. The photographer later filed charges for assault, and some of his supporters intimidated Eric in abusive phone calls, warning him to remove his YouTube documentation of these and related events. How this will end is not entirely clear as this book goes to press.

28. WHO IS DOING THE WORK HERE?

The bad weather continued and few boats arrived. At the previous day's volunteer meeting we had discussed taking the opportunity to continue winterizing the camp. This would include laying down sandbags around Oxy to prevent rain seeping into the tents. In the morning, this plan ran into a few hiccups when the first bags proved too weak, but eventually the sandbag operation got going.

My friend Anne told me a story. An International Rescue Committee bus arrived, and a group of refugees started forming a line, waiting for the bus to depart. Several IRC men stood smoking and waiting. They were also watching Anne, who was bending over an extremely heavy sandbag nearby, trying to load it into a wheelbarrow. She is pretty strong, but after several attempts she was close to giving up. The bag was just too heavy. The IRC men looked on. Suddenly, one of the refugees, unable to stand the sight of her unaided efforts any longer, rushed out of the bus line to help her with the sandbags.

Clearly, the IRC were doing very useful work. They were sending the buses that transported refugees from Oxy to Mytilene. Thank God they were doing so, since only a few months earlier, all the refugees, even small children, were obliged to walk the entire 42 miles from the beach to Mytilene.

The UNHCR too did useful work. They sent the other buses that were occasionally needed to transport rescued refugees from the football field straight to Mytilene. They also contributed two excellent large tents at Oxy, each of which could accommodate 200 people. They provided very warm blankets. Their representatives came to Oxy and held informative meetings for refugees. In addition, they sometimes identified vulnerable people such as those with a disability and minors travelling alone, and ensured that the IRC bus drivers knew about them.

Still, there was (and still is) quite a bit of tension between the volunteers and the major agencies, especially the UNHCR and IRC. The UNHCR often puts out publicity videos that suggest it is doing far more than it actually does. It once referred to the "fleet of minibuses" with which it claimed to be transporting refugees from the north coast to Mytilene. Most of us had never seen a sign of this mysterious fleet, but someone eventually spotted one such minibus. I know that the

UNHCR works all around the world and is badly underfunded. I also believe that all sorts of behind-the-scenes political shenanigans hamper the UNHCR and other major aid agencies and make it harder for them to take a more active role here. But that is no excuse for misrepresentation.

On Monday morning, there were two UNHCR women standing at Oxy, apparently taking stock of what was going on. Since it was quiet, I decided to go into town to buy some things we needed in the food tent. One of the UNHCR women, seeing that I was getting into my car, asked if she could come with me to buy cigarettes. She was new to the north of the island.

"I'm from Communications," she said, as we drove off. I said that was nice, and added that we had our own communications system.

"Would you like me to tell you about how we work here?" she asked.

OK, I'll be frank. If I had had any sense, I would have said: "Oh yes, please!" Now I shall never know what she might have said. Instead, my mind flew back to the volunteer meeting a couple of weeks earlier, when two UNHCR people came to tell us how best to prevent aggression arising at Oxy.

"It is important to issue tickets."

"You must ensure that people stand in line."

"You must be fair."

"You must ensure that people understand why you are doing what you do."

These were all things that Starfish had been doing competently for many months. So competently that there was almost never any aggression at Oxy. The presentation gave me the feeling, and I was far from alone in this, that the UNHCR was pretty arrogant.

So when the UNHCR woman asked me, "Would you like me to tell you about how we work here?" I did not react sensibly. I immediately replied:

"I know exactly what you do here. You provide two nice large tents and very good blankets." The woman was taken aback. She told me that volunteers in Mytilene often did ask for the UNHCR's advice, and this may well be true. I dropped her off, barely managing to suppress my laughter, and went off to do my own shopping.

When I got back to Oxy, I told the camp manager about my encounter. I thought it quite amusing. But she had already heard about it.

"It has caused problems," she said. She did not personally think I was in the wrong, but apparently the communications woman had complained, and the local UNHCR leader was fuming at the lack of respect shown to his worker.

I decided that I needed to defuse the tension a little. I went over to the UNHCR man, but he was talking on his mobile. When he got off the phone, almost an hour later, I went over and apologized, saying that I had meant no disrespect.

(A few weeks later, after I had left Lesvos, the UNHCR posted a video giving the impression that it coordinates the teams of volunteers in the north of the island. Perhaps it was a reference to a meeting it chairs. Although it was amusing to see that I had a tiny part in the video myself, handing out food, I was a little mystified. The kind way to view this version of things would be that it is wishful thinking.)

I set about reorganizing the food tent. The transformation had shuffled the huts into a new constellation. The sandwiches and water were now stacked in a hut that bore signs of its previous incarnations: children's drawings from the period in which it had been used for women and children, and a list of symptoms in Farsi from the time it was the medical tent. It had now metamorphosed into the temporary food tent. Our new carpenter came over to saw a hole in the side to make a window through which we could serve the sandwiches, fruit and drinks.

In this lull, I had time to muse on my role here. Was I actually a useful volunteer? I watched people around me busily engaged in carpentry, cleaning and reorganizing space, and felt a little useless. Then I recalled that I had spent many long days on my feet, serving people sandwiches and fruit. Given my age, I had always planned to avoid engaging in too much physical activity. It was in no one's interest for me to get injured and to need medical attention myself. Still, I started wondering if I was being overly cautious. Who was I to get all high and mighty about the UNHCR?

29. "PLEASE, MA'AM, I'M NOT FULL"

The day started slow, and the absurd phrase, "We have too few refugees" kept popping into my mind. As always, it was unclear whether the slowdown was caused by the direction of the wind or the Turkish coastguard actions, for instance, in response to political pressure from the EU. Clearly, the EU's interests do not run parallel to Turkey's. All the bribes in the world are not going to persuade Turkey to patrol its entire seaboard so effectively that no boats can leave. Every time a coastguard boat escorts one of the dinghies back to the coast, it leaves a gap into which others can put to sea. And the idea that Greece, with its immense coastline, should be stemming the influx of refugees is not just immoral but displays a complete ignorance of the geography of the region. In short, there is no way of stopping the flow, because the refugees are escaping from unspeakable horrors and the boat mafia are running an extremely lucrative business. That morning, reports reached us of a hundred thousand people waiting in the woods near the coast for a sign that they could put to sea.

I worked this shift with a woman with a wry sense of humour, Melanie, from Leeds in Yorkshire, in the northern UK, who had taken a leave of absence from her sales job, having been forced out of the career she loved as a care worker by the abysmal wages in that sector. We engaged in banter about our early lives, and Melanie said:

"Ah well, what doesn't kill you makes you strong."

And I wondered whether this was true of all the refugees who had passed through Oxy over the past months – thousands upon thousands of them. I also mused that Europe was being enriched by some of the strongest, kindest and most energetic people you're likely to meet. How could I convey to people who had not been here my conviction that we needed the refugees as much as they need us?

At one point I was alone in the food tent, and one of our Farsi interpreters came in, a young man who lives in Sweden. Sometimes he felt weighed down by the distressing nature of the stories he had been listening to all day and needed to retreat. Once he seemed receptive to conversation, I asked him about his life: what did he do for a living in Sweden? He told me that he was a professional poker player.

I felt that life was playing something of a

trick on me. My aversion to smoking had already been flattened and made to look petty, and now here was this excellent volunteer, working round the clock with supreme dedication, and he was a poker player! My one remaining prejudice, against professional gamblers, was being squashed too. I told the interpreter that Oxy had stretched my mind and crushed my prejudices to dust. It made him smile.

"Thank you for sharing that with me," he said softly.

Kenny came over, in a state of simmering fury because the electrician had not done his job properly and the lights weren't working. He was trying to sort it out, but sensibly calculated that it was not wise for him to experiment on the wiring by himself.

Some groups of refugees arrived from Eftalou. One teenager came back to the food tent half an hour after getting his ration and said, with disarming simplicity:

"Please ma'am I am not full, can I have an apple?" and for some reason I teared up, as I had done on my first day. It was as if now that I was almost ready to leave, I could afford to let my emotions back in again.

It happened again when I said "Welcome to Europe!" to a man, and he replied,

"Thank you. You too welcome to Syria" and he mimed, "when all this is over."

I said, "If I were a refugee you would help me too," and his reply made my eyes fill with tears. Where had the tears been?

I fetched the last toys and writing materials from my car, and played Santa

Claus to the children in the tent. I gave a doll to a little girl called Ola, handed out a bunch of cars to the little boys. I gave two boys from Iraq, Hamed and Asef, a set of coloured pencils and paper, and their eyes lit up with excitement. A large family from Afghanistan sat around on the floor of the UNHCR tent. They said they were going to Holland.

"I come from Holland!" I said and we all grinned. I wondered if I would see them again.

Back at the apartment I ate my way – yet again – through an entire bag of pistachio nuts. When I had finished, I spied another little green kernel on the floor, picked it up and popped it into my mouth. It squirmed and wriggled around my tongue.

I spat out the green bug, and looked at it. I'm the sort of person that likes to extract lessons from stuff that happens. So what was the takeaway here? Well: first, I was eating far too many pistachios. Second, it was a foul habit to pick something off the floor and stick it into my mouth. Third, perhaps I ought to get my eyes tested to see if my glasses were strong enough. Did the event also, perhaps, have a symbolic significance? Occasionally you find something in your body that you don't want there. Occasionally you hear something that you don't want to hear. About Hitler, for instance.

"Now you're stretching things," said my inner critic.

30. TWO EXTRAORDINARY CHARACTERS

When I arrived at the food tent for my final day's work, an early shift, refugees were just starting to wake up. I had read that 250 had spent the night at Oxy. Soon they would all be wanting breakfast. It was 7 a.m. Entering the food tent, I saw a man lying on the floor, apparently asleep. I thought it might have been someone from the night shift. As the lines were starting to grow, there was no time to wake him up or make enquiries. I set about serving the people who were standing in line for food.

A fellow Starfish came to help and I asked her to find out why there was a man lying on the floor in the food tent. Ten minutes later, she returned with the information that he was paralyzed. That still didn't explain why he was here rather than, say, in the medical tent, but I was too busy to go into it. An hour later the man woke up and sat up to have a cigarette. I suppressed my petty thoughts about smoking in the food tent and gave our guest a sandwich and some milk. He only spoke Arabic, so I had soon exhausted my meagre store of pleasantries. Someone came in and said that the man couldn't be moved until 10 a.m., when the doctors arrived at the medical tent. I tried not to worry about the man needing to go to the toilet.

A little while later, two of our camp managers came in and sat on the floor with the man. Both of them lit up cigarettes. This time I did mumble something about smoking in the food tent, but I felt mean-spirited and out of order.

When I had served everyone breakfast, I had time to turn around and ask about the man. One of the managers spoke good Arabic and told me our guest's history. He had fought with the Free Syrian Army, the moderate rebels supported by the West. Syrian government troops, the troops of President Assad, had come to his family home and made everyone lie down on the ground, after which they had executed them all by firing bullets into their heads. Our guest showed us the wound in his head. The rest of his family was dead. His own bullet had not killed him, but he could no longer walk unaided. He was a warm, quiet man, the kind of person who makes friends easily. People had helped him to get to Turkey and to board a boat to Greece. He had given his life jacket to someone else on the boat because he said it didn't matter if he lived or not. But he had survived, and he was here. Although he had come unaccompanied, an Iraqi family had befriended him They agreed to travel with him on the bus to Moria. In the end I saw him hobbling away, dragging his feet, two of his new friends supporting him on either side. I rushed over to say goodbye to him, and to wish him good luck.

All through the day I thought of this astonishing story, and wondered what the future would hold for this Syrian man, bereft of his family, in Europe.

In the evening I had dinner with my dear Canadian friend John. He had invited two other friends along, and after a while I fell into conversation with one of them, a volunteer with a different group called Z. I soon noticed that Z had an unusually abstract style of speech, picking the bones of every idea until every assumption and bias that might be lurking within it had been laid bare. I was rather in awe of such rigorous analysis. He also applied it to himself, constantly questioning his own thought processes, his own "internal hierarchies." How exhausting! I thought, and I asked him how he had developed such a detached attitude to his own identity. The answer was intriguing and unexpected.

Z's father had been a major drug dealer. Following his arrest and conviction the family had been moved and rehoused under a witness protection scheme. Z was just a boy of twelve. From the city environment in which everyone knew him, and in which his quirks – for he was a quirky kid – were accepted, he was spirited away to a small town. On the day the family arrived, he went out to explore, and immediately got beaten up – twice.

"Couldn't you fight?"

"Oh, I learned to fight after that," he said. He was a nerdy boy, but there was no alternative. He learned, in fact, to be someone else. Here was a man whose identity had literally been deleted and built up again from the ground up. So how surprising was it that he had learned to mistrust all certainties, including his own? So far from jumping to conclusions, Z is that rare individual who allows all the ideas that surface to remain suspended in air, where we can look at them. If we could all do that, learn to think *more slowly*, could we not teach ourselves to become more rational and more compassionate at the same time? Perhaps slow thought is a cousin of slow food: good for the soul. I told Z I would write to him when I encountered difficult philosophical problems. He replied that those were the only kinds of e-mails to which he was likely to respond.

As I returned to the apartment, I felt that in the refugee I had met in the morning, and the volunteer I had met in the evening, I had glimpsed a broader canvas of human possibility than I was accustomed to seeing. I hoped I was the better for it.

31. TO THE BEACH

It was my last day. I planned to do some shopping to take final gifts to the refugees at Oxy. I left the car at the local parking lot, but as I set off up the hill to the shops, I saw a message that a boat was coming in at Eftalou. I decided to go down to the beach instead. Finally. Although I had seen plenty of boats approaching, I had never been to the beach as people disembarked. This was something I ought to have seen at first hand, so I got in the car and drove to Eftalou.

When I got to the beginning of the dirt road, I found Trace and Jenni parked and looking down at the next beach along to the east in a state of shock. It turned out that a large wooden boat had crossed over from Turkey quite quickly. For some reason, no one, including the team staffing the "watch tower," the top room in Hotel Belvedere with the best view of the sea, had spotted it. By the time the mistake was realized, it was too late to send people to help ensure a safe landing. Fortunately, the boat had come ashore on a sandy stretch, and the 140 men, women and children had all clambered out safely without any assistance.

"This is not how it's supposed to happen," said Trace, shaking her head. And Jenni was almost in tears from horror at what might have happened if the landing had gone wrong. I turned towards the refugees, who were starting to troop up the cliff path from the beach where they had landed and down again to the adjacent beach where dry clothes and bottles of water lay waiting for them. Buses would take them from there to Oxy. The refugees were from Iraq, almost all of them Yazidi families fleeing from the massacres in their homeland. Children and women staggered along the path in little groups.

I took the arm of a woman who looked utterly dazed, as if she had found herself transported to another planet. She carried a baby, and held the hand of another small child. A third child walked beside us.

"You have three children?" I tried, as I led the woman along the stony cliff path.

Once she understood, she held up six fingers. Six children. There was no father, as far as I could see. She was clearly exhausted, unable to react, to do anything other than to hold her child and to place one foot in front of another.

I held her arm and guided her as best I could, but I had no words of comfort. I had not learned how to say "You are safe now!" at the food tent.

Once we got down to the beach further west, where supplies lay ready, I looked around to see what I should do. A Yazidi man attracted my attention, wanting me to understand something of the vileness that lay behind them. He pointed to women, first one and then another, and made a forceful wringing and throwing gesture with one hand – whether he was trying to indicate abduction or murder I couldn't tell.

"Five thousand woman!" he said, and I bowed my head.

"I'm so sorry," I said, hearing the small phrase hit the air.

I suddenly remembered I had sixteen pairs of shoes and ten pairs of jogging pants in my car. I had bought them the day before, meaning to put them in the storage at Eric and Philippa's house. Clearly, there was now an immediate use for them. I went over to the car and got them out, lining the shoes up on a tarp on the beach in order of size. Once the refugees noticed them, they were all gone within five minutes. The jogging pants were soon gone, too.

I watched as one of the volunteers sat a woman down, stripped off her wet socks, and starting rubbing her feet with kind competence. As I took this in, I asked myself, not for the first time, why I lacked the ability to engage on this close, physical level. I asked someone who radiated businesslike efficiency what I should do, and she looked at me rather impatiently as if I ought to know.

"You could do something with these baby

carriers," she suggested.

So I fished a colourful folded cloth out of the pile. It bore a label that said "Greetings from Marina from the Achterhoek." A Dutch donation! Then I went in search of a baby. I found a gorgeous smiley baby whose name, I learned, was Angelina. But my incompetence, it seemed, was bottomless here. I was quite clueless as to how the carrying cloth actually worked, so even for this I had to find someone else to help. I collared a person whose hi-vis vest said "Nurse" and asked her to help me. Although she too had no experience with winding a cloth baby carrier, she was of a practical cast of mind and soon worked it out. It was quite roomy, and Angelina would be carried along for the rest of her journey in this comfortable cradle up against her mother's body.

Recognizing that I was pretty useless on the beach, I returned to Molyvos, and set off for the shops. I bought balls, bubble-blowing tubes, cuddly toys, cars, and all kinds of drawing materials for the children. Then I descended the steps of the village one final time.

In the late afternoon I went up to Oxy to say goodbye to Kirsten and others. I also saw Lucas there and went over to him. Our eyes met and we gripped hands.

"I like you," I said.

"I like you too," he replied, and the words hung there quite fresh, as if they were seldom spoken.

I also had to say goodbye to Oxy. I remembered how wretched this patch of land had seemed to me when I first saw it, a sorry parking lot beside the road. Now, a month later, it seemed to me a wonderful place, full of kindness and hope, a true refuge for the weary traveller, overlooking a spectacular view of the sea. I had made friends here, seen the courage of refugees who had lost everything, and seen them off as they continued on their hazardous journey. They now knew themselves safe from bombs and fanatical murderers, but they were facing a whole new range of hardships and hazards. I had also come to know myself better. I knew I was reliable and capable of work demanding resilience to stress and great stamina, but that I had much to learn about engaging with people on a personal level. Language is not the only way to communicate.

That evening I had dinner with Trace, Jenni, and some women who were conducting a fundraising campaign. Towards the end of the evening the Scottish photographer I had met before caught our attention from a nearby table. She was feeling irked about the new way in which volunteers were meeting boat arrivals.

"They're standing too close together, creating a tunnel for the refugees to walk through," she grumbled, "and that means we can't see. We have to walk right up to our knees into the water to get a decent picture."

We tried explaining that the aim was to protect people who were not so steady on their feet after the crossing, to prevent them from falling and to help them to feel safe. The photographer remained unconvinced and saw it as an unnecessary attack on her work.

"You do need us to take pictures. And what you're doing, you know, is putting photographers' lives in danger by forcing us to go out into the water!" she said, without any intended irony.

Trace stayed calm, I don't know how she does it, but I was unable to do so. It seemed to me that the photographer had turned the priorities upside down, and I said so. Later on I mused about this photographer and her strange inversion.

With her straight-faced assertion that volunteers were putting photographers' lives in danger by protecting the refugees, perhaps her attitude was symptomatic of a wider self-centeredness that has infected many European societies. I am referring to the persistent belief that it is Europe that has a crisis. That Europe has a "refugee crisis." In fact, of course, we have an influx of people we could easily absorb if we had the will to do so, and if we had political leaders who were capable of providing moral leadership. It is the people in war-torn countries, people who have been forced to flee for their lives, who are in crisis.

32. WHY GO?

You might have expected to hear a clearer account of my motivation for going to Lesvos at the beginning of this book rather than at the end. But I was hoping to reach people beyond my own small crowd. We all do it, don't we? Congratulate each other on Facebook for causes we share. Repeat the same arguments to people who applaud them. How often do we dare to engage in real dialogue – not abuse – with people who do not agree with us?

My aim in writing this book was partly to document an extraordinary month and pay tribute to the volunteers. A more important aim, however, was to reach out to people who feel vaguely sympathetic to refugees but also, at times, ignorant and uneasy, and who have an open mind.

Having said that, I will now come clean and describe more precisely the feelings and thoughts that prompted me to spend a month volunteering on Lesvos instead of taking a holiday.

As I said at the beginning, I watch the news *a lot*. I saw endless videos of boats arriving. I followed the news as successive European governments erected fences to keep out the flows of refugees and migrants crossing through the Balkan states on their way to northern Europe. Meanwhile, my son-in-law, a TV journalist who works for a Dutch history series, made an episode on the response of the Dutch government to the Jewish refugees trying to enter the country while fleeing from Nazi Germany in the 1930s and during the war. The politicians' concerns looked and sounded horribly familiar:

"There are far too many of them! They will disrupt our society!"

Like many people watching the news on BBC or CNN, I burst into tears at the sight of the lifeless body of three-year-old Aylan Kurdi, face down on a beach, washed up after his family's boat sank in their abortive attempt to reach Europe. The poignant photographs with the little red shoes caused a momentary stirring of conscience around the Western world. It was as if people needed those photographs to realize, "that's a child like my child!" After that I read reports every week of more children drowning in the Aegean Sea, but the media carried no more moving pictures of individual tiny dead bodies, and these children were not named.

As I watched, I became more and more conscious of the fact that I was here, and the desperate people fleeing from the bombing and mayhem were "over there," on the other side of my TV and computer screens. And at the back of my mind, the thought formed that, like Alice through the looking-glass, I could step through the screen to the other side and do something useful there, instead of just staying here, watching in the comfort of my home. The disaster tourist, in one sense at least, is not the person who goes to help but the person who watches a calamity on the TV, feels bad for a few seconds, and then switches off to watch Game of Thrones.

It's the distance, isn't it? If you opened your front door and there was a homeless refugee family standing there in wet clothes, destitute and hungry, most people would drop their plans for the day and take them in. But our screens anaesthetize us. We don't make the leap to think, "Wait, I could go there. It's not impossible." And we don't make the leap to think, "What would I do if I had to leave my home to escape from being killed?"

I recalled the last Syrian man to whom I had said my routine phrase, "Welcome to Europe!" And to whom I had said, "if I were a refugee, you would help me too."

"Yes," he replied, "Of course. But I hope that this never happens to you."

EPILOGUE

"So, did it change your mind about anything?" my friend in Amsterdam asked a month after I arrived home.

"Well, it made me realize how amazing the people of Lesvos are. I had got the impression beforehand that most of the people helping the refugees were foreigners. But that is nonsense. Lots of locals work as volunteers, and some of the hotels and restaurants have been part of the aid effort since the start. We don't hear enough about all the priests and other local people, poor as they are, who bring donations and make sandwiches, who go down to the beaches and take care of refugee children. In fact the Greek fishermen save more lives, perhaps, than anyone else. They are proud, unsung heroes.

"Not unsung any more, surely?"

"You mean the nomination for the Nobel Peace Prize? Yes, it's wonderful that the Greek islanders have been nominated, for their courage and compassion in rescuing and caring for the refugees! They certainly deserve it."

"And do you feel you've done enough now?"

"What do you mean?"

"Well, you said before you left that it wasn't enough to collect warm clothes, to write letters and post things on Facebook and Twitter. So do you feel you've done enough now?"

"What? After handing out a lot of cheese sandwiches and saying 'Welcome to Europe!' a few thousand times? No, of course not!"

"So, what's the point? How does it affect anything? Are you a different person now?"

"All change is made up of tiny bits, isn't it? Whether it's changing yourself or changing the opinions of those around you, bringing pressure to bear on your government, on the EU. Changing the world, it's all ... incremental. I rant less. I try to talk to people who disagree with me without shouting at them."

"So when would you feel you'd done enough?"

"I don't want to feel I've done enough. I want

to feel I'm helping, now. By persuading people to get involved. In whatever way they can. As for us, we're planning our next trip to Lesvos."

"Back to Oxy?"

"No, Oxy has closed now. But Starfish is strong. It does what is needed. It still cares for people who are rescued and brought to the harbour in Molyvos. It works at Moria and in the new camp run by the IRC, and helps to sort and distribute supplies."

"How do you know all that?"

"I read the messages. Every day. Part of me is still there."

The net proceeds from sales of this book will be donated to Starfish.

If you enjoyed reading this book, I hope you will consider posting a brief review on Amazon.

Please consider donating to one or more of the volunteer organizations that are active on the Greek islands in the North Aegean.

For Starfish,
go to http://www.asterias-starfish.org/en/,
which includes a link to the donations page.

You can support the lifeguards at:
http://en.proactivaopenarms.org/
and
http://www.leetchi.com/c/money-pot-lifeguard-hellas-rescue-team

For general information on volunteering on Lesvos, go to http://lesvosvolunteers.com/

If donating goods, please check the list of items needed first. Sorting and clearly labelling donations will greatly help the volunteers receiving them. Eric and Philippa Kempson have a Wish List on amazon.co.uk.

If you have the stamina to look into a truly intractable problem, research the issue of refugees who are often stranded without any help on the military island of Farmakonisi.

Numerous people write incisively about the refugees coming into Europe: e.g. Peter Bouckaert of Human Rights Watch and Nick Malkoutzis of Kathimerini. Many Starfish volunteers, Peggy Whitfield among others, write articles and Facebook posts that can help others to keep abreast of events on the ground, which change rapidly from one week to the next.

Made in the USA
Charleston, SC
26 May 2016